W9-ABC-086

HOW TO MOTIVATE
YOUR CHILD TOWARD SUCCESS

HOW TO MOTIVATE YOUR CHILD TOWARD SUCCESS

WILLIAM STEUART McBIRNIE
B.A., M.R.E., B.D., D.R.E., Ph.D., O.S.J.

Tyndale House
Publishers, Inc.
Wheaton, Illinois

LIBRARY OF CONGRESS CATALOG CARD NUMBER 79-66551
ISBN 0-8423-1528-4, PAPER
COPYRIGHT © 1979 BY WILLIAM STEUART MCBIRNIE
ALL RIGHTS RESERVED
FIRST PRINTING, NOVEMBER 1979
PRINTED IN THE UNITED STATES OF AMERICA

CONTENTS

INTRODUCTION

The most important and potentially the most satisfying task parents could possibly have is to teach their children to be "successful." When children inevitably do fail, in any area of life, parents often feel they themselves have failed at their primary calling.

I would encourage parents not to harbor unnecessary guilt. All parents fail to some degree because they are flawed human beings, as are their children. Sometimes the best possible parents, or the best intentioned parents, will not see their utmost efforts crowned with success. Children are people and in time they grow to be responsible for themselves. If they defy their parents in adulthood, there is little the parents can do.

Nevertheless, good parental teaching and training, if it is begun early enough, can have a tremendous influence upon the child. And it is better to be late than never to begin at all.

This book contains principles based on the author's observations. They will not, perhaps, seem to be in agreement with some widely held theories on child rearing, but the parents who read are urged to reflect on their validity. Herein, I have tried to deal realistically with problems of environment, child motivation, goals, conflicts, ideology, economics, sociology, religion, and sex.

I have seen the reasons for failure in child rearing during forty years as a minister and educator. What I know and believe, I have poured into this book. I sincerely hope it will prove a window of light.

W. S. McBirnie, Ph. D.
California Graduate School
of Theology, Glendale, California

ONE
TEACH
YOUR CHILD
TO BE A
SUCCESS
IN LIFE

Some children grow up to be successful in spite of their parents' indifference or hostility toward them. But this is rare and usually occurs when the child is unusually gifted or has a strong sense of self-reliance. As the world knows, Winston Churchill was grossly neglected as a child, but in adulthood magnificently overcame this handicap. However, the majority of neglected children become failures in adult life. Of course, even the best home training does not absolutely assure success, since children are products of heredity as well as environment.

We should face this truth about children: just as they differ from each other in physical characteristics, they differ in mental and emotional strength. There is an interaction between their physical, emotional, and mental characteristics. A physically strong but mentally weak child will never become an outstanding adult. Likewise, a mentally superior but emotionally maladjusted child will have a hard hill to climb in order to become successful. Similarly, a child who is physically handicapped carries an extra load which he may not overcome.

Nevertheless, all other things being equal, a child *can* be taught success. If he or she is taught *how* to be successful, there is a greater likelihood that the child will become a success.

What is "success"? Can we define it? Can we even describe it? Who is to decide what "being a success" is? Is success like beauty, existing only in the eye of the beholder? Is success comparative or absolute? Can we really measure success? Is it possible to be a success in some aspects of life and not in others? If this last question is capable of an answer, can we ever say that anyone is wholly successful?

Perhaps we can learn what success is by contrasting it with failure. We certainly know what failure is. It is not living up to one's capacity, capabilities, and opportunities. Yet, to some degree, success is determined by the person who is doing the judging.

A son may be a rank failure in the eyes of the world and yet a fond mother may see him as a success. Likewise a person may not succeed in the judgment of man, yet in God's eyes may have achieved greatly. It all depends upon who is doing the judging. Yet we should not unnecessarily complicate the issue.

From a Christian point of view, man's chief end is to glorify God and enjoy him forever (so at least the Shorter Catechism assures us). Perhaps this is correct as far as it goes. But it says nothing about the fulfillment of one's gifts nor the satisfaction and worth of human relationships on earth.

Hence we shall have to define true success more broadly. Perhaps this definition or description may point toward true success: *A person may be said to be successful when he has mastered the purpose of life, fulfilled himself, found identity, achieved self-respect, served his dependents and friends well, supported good causes, developed the ability to keep his commitments, performed socially useful tasks, and discovered the will of God for his brief stay on earth.*

TWO
TEACH
YOUR CHILD
TO KNOW
WHO HE IS

It is surprising how few people ever understand what self-identity is. The painful teen years are troublesome mainly because of a lack of self-identity. The teenager often does not know *who* he is. This thought does not often trouble the child of preteen years because he has not lived long enough nor had enough experiences to become overly introspective. In these early years he is protected and defines himself in terms of his family. Unless his home life is uncertain, he is embarking on a voyage of exciting discovery.

In the teen years, however, family relationships begin to weaken. The teenager has to face society more and more. He is forced to compare and compete. He desperately wants to be accepted and to "belong." Yet he may not have developed the characteristics which are valued by his fellows. To seek approval, therefore, he begins to try to conform to the standards of his peer groups. If their behavior conflicts with what he has been taught, or with the wishes of his parents, the teenager is possessed by morbid thoughts, a sense of alienation, and even rejection. His attitude at home may become resentful, rebellious, and sullen. His deportment is one symbolic act of antagonism and defiance after another. He is constantly testing to see how far he can go without forfeiting whatever he values most.

Hence, wise parental discipline sets limits. Even wiser discipline makes punishment for exceeding those limits self-fulfilling and inherent in the act of defiance itself.

For example, "John, you can use the car this afternoon when you show me your homework is done. But don't expect, or even ask to use it, if the homework is not done." If enforced, this kind of discipline places the young person in potential conflict only with himself and his responsibilities rather than in conflict with his parents. He is not being rejected or denied, or from his point of view being treated unfairly. He understands the rules of the game and has a clear-cut challenge to perform—or he will reap the consequences of his own decisions.

Unconsciously, this need for discipline also bestows a sense of identity. The child under discipline is assured that he belongs to a social unit, the family, in which he has a part; to which social unit he owes obedience and allegiance and from which he gains assurance of who he is (e.g., "I am the son of the Smith family").

Further along, however, he will have to leave the family or at least grow away from it. Who then is he? At this time the loss of self-identity becomes, or can become, very painful.

All people, and even many animals, draw their identities from the groups or individuals, or in the case of human beings, the causes and institutions to which they consciously belong.

"I am *Mrs.* Smith" (i.e., I "belong" to Mr. Smith).

"I am John Smith, *Accountant*" (i.e., I "belong" to the accounting profession or a particular firm of accountants).

"I am Mary Smith, *Secretary to Mr. Jones of the Bank*" (i.e., I "belong" to Mr. Jones and to the bank).

"I am David Smith; *I attend City High*" (i.e., I "belong" to my family and to the high school).

In general, a woman draws her self-identity and defines her chief purpose in life from her husband or children and only secondarily from her employer.

On the other hand, a man generally draws his identity from his work. A man tends to feel prolonged unemployment about as painfully as does a woman the loss of her marriage. In both cases the loss of identity is even more disturbing than the loss of income.

Since the average young person has not yet found the persons, causes, or institutions to which he will "belong," he is liable to be disturbed and unfulfilled, hence unhappy and prone to melancholy or unusual behavior.

The most frequent reason for unsuitable marriages is often the sheer desire to "belong" to someone at any price, as soon as possible, so as to escape the prolonged uneasiness of not knowing *who* one is.

It is this very matter of self-identity which causes many men to be so overly absorbed in their work. They may tell themselves, and to a degree be honest, that they are working hard *for their family's* welfare. But why do they *continue* to work so hard, and frequently absent themselves from the family they profess to be working for, when they reach a high level of economic success? The obvious answer is, they are not working *for the family* as they profess to be, but for continuance of their own self-identity.

Again incidentally, this explains why retired people, especially men, are often very unhappy even when they no longer have financial problems. Retirement may mean financial ease but it certainly means some loss of identity, and this is frequently a shattering or depressing experience.

This is one of the reasons that a fervent Christian faith bestows a strong sense of self-identity. "I am God's child" (i.e., "I belong to God, who is the all-wise Guide and Father. He will lead me to the right person and the right career"). How very fortunate is the youth who has this firm belief to assist him in the difficult teen years.

All of this tells us much about young people and the subconscious reason for their increase of problems as they reach the teen years. If they can be given help to find self-identity, to know who they are, to some degree, many of their problems can be reduced.

THREE
TEACH
YOUR CHILD
AN AWARENESS
OF CONSEQUENCES

From any beginning I can recall, I was always a liar, a sneak, a braggart, a show-off and a thief. . . . I was unable to calculate consequences. False Starts: A Memoir of San Quentin and Other Prisons *by Malcolm Braly, Little, Brown.*

One attribute of maturity which youth often lacks is an awareness of consequences. How could it be otherwise? How could we expect young people, who have not had many of life's vital and transforming experiences, to be always aware of what the consequences of their decisions will be? That kind of understanding comes only by experience and learning. Learning about anything includes becoming aware of the consequences which follow decisions.

Cleverness or even logic cannot provide a total awareness of the probable consequences of one's decisions and actions. Human beings are not primarily creatures of logic. We often suppose we *reason* when what we actually do is *feel*. Emotions are enemies of logic and they often blind us so that we cannot see what is coming. Our strong feelings *demand* satisfaction *now!* All emotions by nature have an urgency, an immediacy, about them. They are, therefore, unsafe guides for youth in times of decision making.

It is the glory and crown of age that it has at last learned to be aware of consequences. But, for the young, this must be an acquired skill. A young person who learns this secret early will be far ahead of the crowd.

Develop an awareness of consequences is the greatest *rule for living* there is. Show me a person who has effectively developed an awareness of consequences and I will show you a person who has found the real secret of success. It is the irresponsible or immature person who lives only for *now,* who is moved primarily by his feelings and their spirit of immediacy. It is the wise man who knows what consequences mean, and who is able to predict them and to discipline his life by the knowledge until he achieves his goals. A person unconcerned about consequences will not have goals, nor will he steer toward objectives. He will drift and never realize until it is too late that not deciding is, in itself, a decision!

HOW TO FAIL

Is there a sure prescription for failure? There is, and it is simple! *Act as if there were no such things as consequences,* and you will fail every time. Live for the moment. Have no awareness that the seeds you sow today will bring a harvest tomorrow, whether for good or ill. Act as if tomorrow will never come.

Look at any juvenile delinquent; go to any courthouse; observe the trial of any young person in trouble, and what will you see? Invariably, inevitably, you will find that such a young person has not learned to accept the fact that there are consequences to his decisions. He has never learned to look ahead. What he wants, he wants *now.* If what he wants now interferes with his education, then education loses out. He may feel he can earn more money at some job *now,* independent of schooling; so he'll sacrifice his education and take the job! Never mind the future consequences. Too many students follow this shallow philosophy and the results are tragic and chaotic. Those who do not know where they are going, inevitably go wrong.

CAPITALISM AND SOCIALISM

When we analyze the matter, is not socialism basically an *organized* political attempt to allow people to avoid the results of their wrong choices? Socialism says, "Let a person live for today, without self-discipline, without self-sacrifice, without saving." When the exigencies of life catch up with him, as they eventually will, socialism promises that the economic results of his folly will *be offset by the State.* In other words, "Someone else will pay the price if I refuse to do so." Of course, the price for all is to lose freedom and the opportunity of great achievement, for socialism always exacts its payment with interest.

The basic idea behind capitalism is *foresight,* looking ahead, going without, saving money, investing *today* so that *tomorrow* one may be more secure, useful, and happy. Capitalism as a system depends upon personal virtues (although not all capitalists are virtuous in all things or at all times). The appeal of socialism is based upon waste, sloth, and an undisciplined desire to live only for the present. "Let tomorrow take care of itself," says the person duped by socialism. This is one of its evils—that it tries to evade the iron laws of consequence which exist for the moral and personal benefit of mankind. It can do this only by penalizing those who *have* saved and invested. Thus, socialism rides to power by assuring people that they can avoid the consequences of ir- responsibility. They cannot, of course, but socialism temporarily deceives them by assuring them that they will *not* reap what they have sown.

In America, certainly, and probably in the entire world, anyone who lives by the principle of developing an awareness of consequences *can* amass some capital, and by self-discipline can assure eventual financial security and prosperity. Socialism is immoral because it ignores consequences and makes plunder of the prudent *legal,* although it cannot make it right or moral.

JESUS TAUGHT THE NEED FOR AN AWARENESS OF CONSEQUENCES

Notice how Jesus' famous "Sermon on the Mount" is imbued with this philosophy. Jesus said on that occasion, in effect, "Look ahead at the results of your choices. Count the cost of giving your attention to earthly things alone." What did Jesus mean? What is the one constant fact about earth? That *nothing is constant.* Is that too philosophical? Let's put it this way: the only thing changeless about earth is the fact that everything is changing. The mountains are slowly eroding; the seas evaporate and their shorelines move; men are born; they mature; they die; old institutions crumble; old landmarks are torn down. The only thing that is permanent in this world is the fact that nothing is permanent.

"Look, therefore, at the consequences of this fact." Jesus said. "Lay not up for yourselves treasures upon earth, where moth and rust doth corrupt, and where thieves break through and steal: But lay up for yourselves treasures in heaven, where neither moth nor rust doth corrupt, and where thieves do not break through nor steal: For where your treasure is, there will your heart be also" (Matt. 6:19, 20). How do your children's decisions match with what Jesus said?

Many individuals make decisions each day which obviously ignore the dire consequences of choosing a wholly materialistic life, a life from which they must shortly depart. Why then are so many people engrossed in material things? Because they are not wise. A wise man is one who has a sense of values, and he is aware of the penalties of ignoring proper priorities and consequences in his choices. When you are in trouble and call for a wise man, you want the person with the *foresight* to guide you out of your difficulty. This foresight will have been based upon hindsight and insight; wisdom gained by realizing that every decision we make inevitably brings consequences. This is the lesson of history, the lesson of wisdom, and the lesson of the future. The need of every young person is to learn this lesson.

Jesus said:

> Whosoever cometh to me, and heareth my sayings, and doeth them, I will show you to whom he is like:
> He is like a man which built an house, and digged deep, and laid the foundation on a rock: and when the flood arose, the stream beat vehemently upon that house, and could not shake it: for it was founded upon a rock.
> But he that heareth, and doeth not, is like a man that without a foundation built an house upon the earth; against which the stream did beat vehemently, and immediately it fell; and the ruin of that house was great (Luke 6:47-49).

What is the outcome of building upon sand, or the result of building upon rock? Inevitable, inexorable consequences! You may even construct the same type of house, but what is the ultimate difference? It is the *destiny* of the house, built into it at the time when the builder makes his choices. The wise builder looks into the future and sees the stormy weather beating upon his foundation. He knows in advance (because he is aware of consequences) how the sand is going to react and how the rock is going to hold up. So if he is prudent he builds his house upon the rock.

No person is urged by Jesus Christ even to become a Christian until he first looks at the consequences. How do you become a Christian? By first looking at the consequences of your choices. For example, you ask, "Who am I?" The answer, you realize, is, "I am an immortal soul, made in the image of God. I am not just a cultured animal. I am not merely a biological being, but a human being made in the image of the divine Being. I have a spiritual destiny. A million years from now I will be somewhere. I not only *have* a soul; I *am* a soul. God breathed into me the breath of life." You then reflect, "Yet I realize that God is holy, and I am sinful. If I persist in my rebellion, if I persist in saying, 'No, no, no!' to God, the time will come when God will say, 'No, no, no!' to me. Lest that fearful time come, I must *now* make my peace with God. Indeed, he has already made peace with me, and has sent his Son to announce that peace. If I will accept and receive him as Lord, Master, and Savior, the transaction will be complete. My life will become meaningful. My position will be changed from a child of the human race to that of a child of God."

One should consider the consequences of becoming a Christian, and vice versa—the consequences of not becoming a Christian. This is called in the Bible, "counting the cost." Here is a biblical illustration of that truth:

> And a certain scribe came, and said unto him, Master, I will follow thee whithersoever thou goest.
> And Jesus saith unto him, The foxes have holes, and the birds of the air have nests; but the Son of man hath not where to lay his head (Matt. 8:19, 20).

The man had said in effect to Jesus, "I want to become one of your disciples; I want to enroll in your school." "Allright," said Jesus, "come ahead, but first be reminded of the consequences of your decision." Jesus never pulled the wool over anyone's eyes. He stressed, "Before you follow me, *count the cost.* I am not trying to fool you. I am not trying to make it appear easy." He warned, "Don't be under any illusions; there *is* a price that has to be paid. Don't try to follow me unless you are ready to pay it!"

Jesus did not overemphasize the cost because that would have made his way seem one of self-punishment. Neither did he under-emphasize it. He simply requires people to consider it. Remind your children frequently of what the Bible says about the Law of Consequences.

Every exhortation in the Scriptures is based upon the principle: "Consider the consequences!" Typical of what we mean is the recurring biblical admonition: "Come to God, because if you do not, someday it will be too late. Turn your back upon sin, because sin [your own self-will] is an acid which corrodes the soul and will someday eat down to the quick. Already the results of self-will and its bad consequences are evident, but a cure awaits you! Surrender your will, yourself, your ego, to God!"

Only when the Holy Spirit creates within people an awareness of consequences do they become hungry for God. Otherwise, they are indifferent. They will have no keen awareness of spiritual consequences, or, if they do, they will not accept their validity and may ignore them. This they can do for a *time*, but not forever, because not accepting Christ as Savior also has its eternal and final consequences.

Christianity is always concerned with the future. Jesus urged rebels against God to carefully consider the consequences. He commanded Christians to be good stewards now, for the sake of the future as well as the present.

You would, therefore, expect Christianity to prophesy about the future. Not surprisingly, one third of the Bible *is* prophecy. How could it be otherwise? A faith which is based upon reality is necessarily based upon an awareness of consequences. It must, therefore, have foresight. Foresight and wisdom should be revealed in prophecy—and so it is.

Do not let your children think of prophecy as something occult, unscientific, or unsophisticated in this "learned" age. The prophe-cies of the Scriptures are the natural outflow of the very nature of Christianity. If it has genuine foresight, it is aware of con-sequences. If it is aware of consequences, it is going to prophesy. And the prophecies are going to sound like this: "The soul that "sinneth, it shall die." "Whatsoever a man soweth, that shall he also reap." Prophecy is heaped upon prophecy in the Scriptures.

The Bible foretells what is going to happen to nations, to churches, to individuals. The consequences it plainly predicts for each of them, therefore, can assist them in choosing the correct path.

Why did the Son of God spell out so clearly for us the final results of disobedience as well as the rewards of obedience? Because, out of his heart of love, he would have us look ahead that we might choose the rewards that lead to joy, not sorrow. He affirmed:

> These things have I spoken unto you, that my *joy might remain in you,* and that your joy might be full (John 15:11).

The Bible never fails to spell out for us the results of the ways men may foolishly devise for themselves. In case history after case history, in God's great record book of human behavior, we are shown how men have always suffered the penalty and effects of their self-willed actions and choices. Cause and effect follow each other as surely as night follows day, from generation to generation, forever.

NO EXCEPTIONS

Throughout God's Word, we read the sad story of people who have believed that God's laws would make an exception for them. The man who steals is determined to prove that the admonition, "be sure your sin will find you out," does *not* apply to *him.* The man who works seven days a week, fifty-two weeks a year, without serving God, is attempting to show that "six days shalt thou labor" was not commanded for such an exceptional man as he. By every folly ever devised, mankind has tried to disprove God's statement, "Be not deceived; God is not mocked: for whatsoever a man soweth, that shall he also reap" (Gal. 6:7), but in vain!

Concerning the inevitability of consequences, Ralph Waldo Emerson observed:

> This Law writes laws of the cities and nations. It will not be balked of its end in the smallest iota. It is in vain to build or

plot or combine against it. Life invests itself with inevitable conditions, which the unwise seek to dodge. If he escapes them in one part, they attack him in another more vital part. If he has escaped them in form, and in appearance, it is that he has resisted his life, and fled from himself, and the retribution is so much death.

All things are double, one against another. Tit for tat; an eye for an eye; give and it shall be given you. He that watereth shall be watered himself.... What will you have? quoth God; pay for it and take it. It is thus written, because it is thus in life!

Compensation, Ralph Waldo Emerson

For this reason, Christians, of all people, should live not only for today but for tomorrow; for they know what tomorrow will bring. Christianity has taught them consequences!

Christians should not worry about the future as others do. They know that even when life's path temporarily goes underground into the grave, it emerges on the other side as the result of their decision to surrender to God now.

It is this "eternity awareness" which gives Christianity the ability to help its followers to understand who they are and where they are going. Real Christians have an awareness of their destiny and purpose. They do not wander aimlessly as others who have no compass, who do not know how things are going to come out in the end.

Christianity, with its tremendous awareness of consequences, gives to all men who will accept Christ *foresight* concerning that which is to come. It urges them to make good decisions now for a happy future. It warns them to avoid wrong decisions lest they reap a miserable harvest.

Jesus cautioned the bigoted and blind Pharisees of his day, telling them, "You stand at the top of cultured society. Scholastically, you have the best education of anyone these days, and in *natural* things you are very wise. For example, in the afternoon, when the sky is red, you rightly say, 'Tomorrow will be a fair day.' When the morning sky is red, you say, 'the consequences of this portend a foul day.' Oh, you hypocrites! You can so wisely analyze the face of the sky and read its signs, *but you cannot read the signs of the times!*" In effect he accused them of being cultural sophisticates and spiritual idiots. He affirmed, "You cannot see the important spiritual consequences of your decisions. Therefore you don't know what time it is!"

Teach your children that their greatest need in the world today is to constantly be aware of consequences. It is the key to the mystery of life, and to the beckoning, open door of success. The hour is very late and you have not a moment to lose. They have only one life. It is soon over. Why let them waste it? Teach them to weigh the consequences of every decision.

FOUR
TEACH
YOUR CHILD
FREE
ENTERPRISE

No amount of training in the handling of material things, even according to the rules of capitalism and free enterprise (the economic virtues which have made America a marvel of wealth and productivity), can take the place of *spiritual guidance.* A Christian home is the best gift parents can give their children, one to be infinitely valued. Life is too short and eternity too long for the distorted stress we place on lengthy preparation for *this life,* while at the same time giving little time and thought toward training for life after death, which is forever.

True spiritual life is both "caught" and "taught." So are patriotism, love of freedom, respect for personal rights to property, and all the important ideological values which Americans have traditionally treasured.

A child first learns either personal enterprise or socialism at home and in the school. Instruction in capitalism and free enterprise cannot begin too early. Indeed, this training will be started by wise parents in their children's formative years. How a parent teaches his child at six and seven years of age will determine to a large measure how well or poorly the child will function (economically speaking) when he grows to maturity. Whatever his age, the time to begin is *now.*

Socialism often ensnares Christians who have a mistaken idealism. They may look at the short-term "benefits" of welfarism and be blind to its long-term evils. The effect of socialism on such an important value as individualism is disastrous. Socialism stunts the creative capacity of the most gifted. It should be opposed in its practice even in its disguised forms in the home.

Many persons who despise socialism in government, practice it at home without realizing they are creating socialist attitudes in their own children. When their children fall for socialism in their college years, many capitalist-minded parents are astonished at the awful change college has produced. They need not wonder; they, themselves, through ignorance, laid socialistic foundations in the home.

DR. GEORGE CRANE'S ADVICE

Dr. Crane, M.D., Ph.D., writes a popular syndicated column on family and personal problems. This outstanding authority has challenged one of the most ingrained and harmful American practices—that of *giving* children a weekly allowance. Perhaps what he says will shock you. Dr. Crane's formula for successful child rearing (in terms of economic matters and creating in the child a dedication and devotion to free enterprise) is not hard to grasp. In one of his columns he has written:

> It isn't just "liberal" college profs who are making Socialists and Communists out of our youth but the failure of parents to indoctrinate those young people properly BEFORE they meet atheistic, liberal instructors.

> CASE Z-204: Sydney Harris is a popular newspaper columnist.
> Recently he deplored the fact that many parents try to get their children into the so-called "best colleges." Yet, he added, those same colleges often send back those young men and women as arch foes of the economic, political and religious ideals of their own parents.
> "Dr. Crane," I am often asked, "why do the wealthy college educated children of staunch American patriots, then espouse Communism and Socialism?
> "Their own dads often rose from poor boys to become

heads of great department stores and corporations. It was due to our wonderful 'free enterprise' system.

"In fact, the very money that supports those young men in luxury at college, came from their dads' businesses, yet the sons will advocate Communism or Socialism, which are both trying to sabotage 'free enterprise.'

"Dr. Crane, it doesn't make sense, does it?"

"Yes, it makes sense, if you delve beneath the surface! For those same fathers and mothers often failed as parents! They were guilty of one or all of the following common faults of many country club members:

(1) "They themselves learned the hard way that money stands for sweat, toil, calluses and deprived play time. But such experiences are NEVER hereditary, so their children needed to acquire at first hand that same attitude toward money. But those parents then grew overly indulgent so they shelled out large 'allowances' to their youngsters.

"'Easy come; easy go,' thus became the casual attitude of their children toward money. Instead of realizing coins and paper bills really represent minted human life, the kids squandered it on juke boxes or slot machines, sport cars and speed boats.

"They had never actually earned enough to fill the gas tank, but their parents let them live like kings!

(2) "The parents failed to use the 'expressive' or 'persuasive' strategy in teaching those youngsters about 'free enterprise.' Instead of patiently showing the children exactly why 'free enterprise' beats Communism and Socialism, they pontificated and browbeat.

"They shouted in apoplectic rage at the alienisms, instead of listing the specific sales points for our American system.

"But smooth talking college professors then adopted the smiling, persuasive method and thus sold those college youth on the Communist or Socialist 'line'!

(3) "The parents failed their children religiously. Yet all youth have an innate desire for altruism.

"So Communism and Socialism became substitute religious outlets through which those college youth sublimated their inherent yearning to do something constructive.

(4) "Many youth espouse radical ideas just because they hunger for headlines! Thus, they champion stupid causes to get their names in the papers or their faces on TV!"

Probably Dr. Crane has set off howls of anguish from thousands of teenagers who have grown accustomed to living off the family dole. Yet sober reflection indicates that he is right. I have often counseled with parents of ungrateful, rebellious teenagers who feel that a weekly allowance, cars, and charge accounts of their own are their *just* share of the family income.

"After all," the youngsters have fallaciously reasoned, "my job is to go to school; Dad's job is to make the living for the family. It is only *just* that he divide his income with me as well as with Mother."

Up to a point, that reasoning may be sound, especially during children's preschool years. It may also be partially correct when a child faces an emergency. But to freely provide such valuable commodities as clothes, cars, and spending money as their *due* is positively harmful to youngsters in their teens, no matter how financially able the parents are.

Early in life, the child should be taught to associate money and what it will buy with *work*. You cannot expect small children to earn their clothing, of course. As the child matures, however, the wise parent does less and less for him in a direct way, and sees to it that the child can earn more and more. To be sure, children often do sloppy work at first, and their earned income may amount to an allowance for all practical purposes. But the parent has fixed in the child's mind firmly the cause and effect relationship of *work* to *income*.

Dr. Crane mentioned that if the plan is to work, *no ceiling should be placed on the child's income,* provided he does the work. Parents should accept the risk that the child may become industrious and earn more than his allowance would have amounted to. But to successfully encourage systematic and regular work habits is a great gain, and the few extra dollars a month it may cost are the best investment a wise parent can make.

When the limitations on a child's income *depend upon him,* and not upon a fixed amount or allowance, the child is encouraged to believe in the system of free enterprise, capitalism, and personal initiative. This one point alone is the entire heart of the matter.

QUALIFICATIONS OF THIS PLAN

No child who has been trained to relate his income directly to his work can grow up believing society owes him a living. No child who is permitted to earn a bicycle (or later his own car) can blame his parents if he has been given a chance to earn these benefits and has failed to do so.

Parents, of course, must be careful to make things neither too easy nor too hard. "Too easy" means that the serious purpose of this plan becomes a mockery. "Too hard" means that the child will rebel against the whole system. You may be sure that the child will come to you as a parent with tales of how easy *other* youngsters have it by not having to earn but simply to enjoy their allowances. In the long run, however, your child will have gained a sense of self-respect that the others may never know. When your child is older, he will thank you, and he will not fall for the temptations of welfare state mentality.

It is obvious that some families cannot afford to pay the incomes that older children are capable of earning. Their home duties should be paid for at set rates, but they should also be encouraged to take part-time employment outside the home.

SHOULD A CHILD BE PAID FOR ALL WORK?

A child should not be paid for any work in the home which directly affects his own well-being or is part of his immediate concern. Certain tasks, such as cleaning up his own room, caring for pets, doing homework, or running small errands should not require payment. These tasks should be done because the child owes them to the family.

But established responsibilities should be set up as areas of earning. Washing windows, mowing the grass, cleaning the house, painting, repairing, major moving, major errands, gardening, etc., should be paid for. These are not the child's immediate, personal responsibility, and they offer a good opportunity to furnish the youngster with work for which he can be paid, so as to earn his own way.

The child should be paid, not on an hourly rate, but on the basis of each individual task. The hourly wage encourages dawdling. Example: One mother sticks a dime to each window with adhesive tape. When the window is washed, the dime belongs to the child. This trains a child to work fast and efficiently.

Many parents give an allowance and then require a certain amount of general work around the house. This is a self-defeating way to go about training. True, the child may learn to manage money, but he will not and he cannot directly relate a job well done to his own financial prosperity. His allowance (dole) is in practice *his*, no matter how hard or how halfheartedly he works. It is easier to take the money for granted and to lack interest in giving up outside activities in order to work.

In fact, he may resent being forced to work, and get out of it as often as he can invent an excuse. He learns to wheedle or outwit his parents. He would be upset if his allowance were cut down, but may be only too happy to get out of his regular tasks if he can.

COLLEGE

Many parents sacrifice a great deal, over many years, to *send* their children through college. For the young person, the result may be a vacation of sorts, for four years or more, all expenses paid. Worse, the young person may lack gratitude, and in many instances actually waste his time in college. Too often he does not develop an appreciation for higher education, since it costs him nothing except time and study.

Perhaps students should not be required to work at a job full time, *plus* carrying a full school load. But they should save a part of their earnings for some years before college, and if possible should take a part-time job while in school. They will then value their education, since they have contributed to it. Parents should never totally subsidize the young person's college education, no matter how financially able they are.

Children should not be bribed to go to college. Instead, they should be shown the economic advantage of a college education in their own self-interest. The income of a typical college graduate over a lifetime is about $100,000 above that of the average non-college graduate. This should encourage the child to strive and help earn his own way.

PRACTICAL GUIDES FOR ACTION

Many parents feel somewhat ashamed that they cannot do more for their children. They try to make up for this by lavishing love upon them. They wait on them hand and foot and thus try to compensate. This is both unnecessary and unwise, for children should share in all of the family's limitations, except when they are very young.

When children are young, it is admittedly easier for parents to wash dishes or sweep floors than to train the children to do these tasks. Unfortunately, many parents continue to wait on their children until they mature in years but have failed to mature in responsibility. Training a child to work skillfully is one of the parents' most important and rewarding tasks.

Some parents wait on their children out of a sense of false guilt. The results of this kind of foolish or shortsighted action are that the child feels useless, fails to grow toward responsible adulthood, and turns to indolence in later years.

A baby receives so much attention, especially when he is the only child or the youngest in the family, that he becomes subconsciously convinced that the world centers around him. Childhood training is supposed to convince him through experience that this is not the case.

But when the parents fondly wait on the child they keep him *childish*—a monstrous thing! All children by nature are irresponsible. They must be taught and trained to accept responsibility. The words "maturity" and "responsibility" are almost synonymous. The earlier the child develops self-reliance and responsibility, the earlier he matures in the right way. We call a youngster *mature* when he accepts responsibility early in life.

Probably some parents unconsciously *want* to keep their offspring childish, hence dependent on them. This is often true when the parent has no other fulfillment in life than parenthood. One must feel pity for the emotionally crippled whose significance in life all hinges on parenthood, and who see their significance slipping away when their child finally starts to leave the nest.

A child who is incapable of work himself may compensate by becoming a tyrant, a "lord" or "lady" who orders his servant-parent about. The young woman who cannot cook or sew, the young man who cannot use tools or paint or mow the lawn, is to be pitied. He or she has been robbed of capability and will secretly feel inferior all his life, possibly taking this incapability out in hostility.

Some parents enjoy "martyrdom." A father often avoids being a real person by convincing himself he is working himself to death primarily to provide for his family, when, in fact, he is actually afraid to face his personal insecurities. People are not put into life merely to become biological reproducers of themselves. Reproduction is only one of the important phases of life. It is not the end of life. "Man's chief end is to glorify God and enjoy him forever," says the catechism. People should live for God, for country, for service, for fulfillment of their talents, as well as for their spouses and their children.

Too many parents have made gods out of their children. This is the worst idolatry, for it perverts parenthood and corrupts the child himself. Children are children—future adults, not gods.

Children must be taught that the world will not wait on them, and if they grow up to be slobs or snobs it will neither tolerate nor reward them.

SHOULD CHILDREN BE REWARDED FOR GOOD GRADES?

All people can be divided into two groups: those who are basically consumers and those who are mainly producers. The child in his earliest years is only a consumer, but he should be taught as soon as possible to be a producer. Above all, he should never be rewarded for consuming, or unconsciously he may be convinced that life will continue to reward him as he consumes more and more, which is the opposite of the truth. A mature person has the privilege of consuming only when he has earned that privilege by producing. That is what the Bible means when it says, "If a man does not work, neither shall he eat."

A child who is rewarded for consuming, whether it be the consumption of food or facts, develops an appetite for self-centeredness. Many children, rewarded by anxious parents for eating, grow obese because they associate eating with approval. Others, rewarded artificially for learning, become bookworms and stay in college or academic surroundings too long. They have associated reward with consumption of learning, and unconsciously have desired to stay in the comfortable surroundings of the school.

This principle will doubtless be a stunning revelation to many parents. But they should not dismiss it as nonsense simply because it is new to them. Remember, a socialist society is primarily a *consuming* society. A free enterprise society is primarily a *producing* society. A child becomes a socialist psychologically before he becomes one politically. The parents' task is to see that the child learns the folly of such a path very early in life.

FIVE
TEACH
YOUR CHILD
PATRIOTISM

Have you recently attended some event, or watched one on television, at which the "Star-Spangled Banner" was played? If so, you may have been quite disturbed, perhaps ashamed, by the behavior of many of those in attendance. Very few people stand at attention, alert, hand over heart, in reverence toward their national flag. Most people slouch, fidget, look about, continue talking, and seem to think the anthem ceremony quite unnecessary. At sports events the general attitude seems to be: "Let's get this over and get on with the game." Some of the high-salaried players seem even more bored than the spectators.

Several years ago we professed to be celebrating the two-hundredth anniversary of our independence. But were we really celebrating? Are we truly grateful?

Some people were thrilled by a ringing challenge from President Kennedy at his inauguration: "Ask not what your country can do for you; ask rather what you can do for your country!" It is dramatic rhetoric and has often been quoted. But how much have we seen it honored by action? Very little. Instead, some inferior slogans which survive today are:

Do your own thing.
Get yours while the getting's good.
Everybody else is doing it—why not you?

In other words, the question is not what is right but what is popular. Cheating isn't cheating if "everyone is doing it." Lying, stealing, breaking laws, obscenity, nudity, self-indulgence, all are OK as long as there is enough of it going on. And of course, what you see on TV or in the movies or read about in the papers must be all right.

Perhaps the most terrible blow to moral standards in our time was the declaration of certain leaders of the sixties that persons were permitted to disobey laws they felt were unjust. It seemed very noble when applied to laws that were really unjust. But as is always true of subjective moral creeds, the edict that we are free to choose which laws we will obey and which we will not, was corrupted into a personal license to do what one pleased.

By this standard, anyone was free to disobey the draft laws, and, moreover, to interfere with their administration: breaking into offices, destroying records, counseling and hiding draft dodgers, etc. Even many clergymen were led into this kind of immoral behavior. By this standard one was free to protest, demonstrate, march, riot, bomb, commit arson, interfere with lawful authorities, desecrate the flag, destroy property, and even take actions which in less permissive times would have been considered treason.

Today the greatest danger to our young people—to young people anywhere—is communism. Not merely the Communist Party, but the concepts of communism and its seductive and subtle influence. The virus of communism is spread not only by Communist Party members. It is spread far more widely by subversives, dupes, fellow-travelers, foolish teachers, writers, media people, and even some of the clergy, who have been taken in by its promises of equality, social justice, and "people's causes."

Communists are the world's greatest masqueraders—the world's greatest makeup artists. They disguise their tyranny, their murderousness, their godlessness, and their plans for world conquest with masks and costumes of respectability. They approach young people as humanitarians, as pacifists, as advocates of equality, democracy, and tolerance; as reformers, idealists, and champions of the oppressed and disadvantaged.

Would you expect them to do otherwise? Communists are not stupid. They are masters of the techniques of propaganda—which means lies and deception and trickery and subterfuge and subversion. They are the most skillful practitioners of the wiles of the devil who have ever infested this earth. So they do not come to young people showing their blood-stained hands. They do not come flaunting their crimes and unspeakable horrors. No, they come as prophets, as deliverers, as rescuers, as kindly and gentle folk interested only in the plight of their fellowmen.

THE PRECISE METHODOLOGY OF THE COMMUNIST PARTY

The Party has asked the question, "How can we destroy the will to resist communism within many young people?" The Communists set about to research means by which they could neutralize the anti-communism of a whole generation of youth.

In these studies, Moscow-trained psychologists dealt with these questions: "What kind of a person within the United States will be most likely to accept communism?" It became apparent that: (1) Children are not politically aware. (2) The older generation is too busy paying bills and raising families. (3) Their converts, then, must come from the naturally rebellious teenagers of the high school or college age bracket.

An equally important study was made of the question, "What *kind* of young person could be so molded by social forces that he would not resist communism?" Such a person would have all or some of the following characteristics:

(1) IMMORALITY. An immoral person is not likely to have moral indignation toward the evils of communism. Because he himself is guilty of evil, he is slow to condemn any kind of evil. It would be necessary for communism to encourage immorality, and to get youth leaders who would approve of immorality. Immorality must become the "in" thing.

One specific illustration of communist involvement with immorality is the Communist Party's own revelation regarding how the Reds see pornography. *Documents on the Cinema,* published under the authority of the Italian Communist Party, discusses films being produced which "arouse sexual feelings, while taking cover under the pretext of art. . . ."

> Nevertheless, these bourgeois, cynical and irresponsible though they be, are fighting our cause. They are, in fact, like

ants working for us without knowing it and without our paying for it, for they devour the very roots of bourgeois society. Why should we throw obstacles in their path? Our interest is to encourage such plays and, by the same token, to be ready to proclaim the agents who create them as champions of artistic liberty. . . .

For tactical reasons, our object is to defend every pornographic enterprise, entirely free from the restrictions imposed by the laws of common morality, while presenting its work as the logical result of the complete artistic freedom so much in vogue today. It is our duty to pursue this policy resolutely. (Quoted in *The National Register,* April 20, 1969.)

(2) CONFUSION. If a person is confused he will have no goals and be unable to resist a movement that knows very well where it is going. For communist purposes it is well to find some youth leaders who speak out for one principle or form of action, and others who propagandize for the opposite. Their followers then become confused; they do not know which leaders to follow; they do not know where the truth lies. The result will be that they will reject any particular aim or goal, and in their confusion they become the ideal person to drop all endeavors, *leaving leadership to communists who have specific goals and objectives.*

(3) WEAKNESS. If communists are to enlist the weak person they must encourage anything that weakens him. They must *applaud* his weaknesses. The weak secretly admire the strength of purpose of the powerful, and so they will not stand up to the superior strength of the communists.

(4) IGNORANCE. The ignorant person is easily manipulated. A lie told to him with great assurance will be believed, especially when the lie is in regard to a subject with which he can identify. So the communists will talk about poverty to the poor, condemning the affluence of the rich.

We see, then, the kind of person who will not offer resistance to communism: an immoral, confused, weak, and ignorant person. How do communists turn the members of a whole generation into this type of people?

In the brightest nation of earth—America—the nation with the most schools, churches, scientific knowledge, and industry, how could the younger generation be led to become such pawns?

(1) DRUGS. The widespread use of drugs is destroying the character of many of our young people, leaving them weakened physically, mentally, and psychologically. In a recent column by Ann Landers a young woman's letter was published:

> The guy I love is on pot. It is making a vegetable out of him and a nervous wreck out of me. When we first met, Steve was a top student. He had a magnetic personality and a thousand friends.
>
> About eight months ago, he became sloppy in his appearance and he seemed to lose his sense of humor. He turned into an argumentative bully and got into trouble with everyone. I knew something was wrong when he started to skip class and forget where we were supposed to meet. One night he fell asleep during a play which I found fascinating. The following day he confessed that he had been on marijuana for nearly a year. Steve dropped out of school in April. His motivation is gone. He is confused and disoriented. I cannot reach him. I am not asking for advice, Ann, I know what I must do. I can't save him, so I must save myself. The purpose of this letter is to support your testimony that marijuana is bad news.

There you have an example of the results of drug usage, and an example of why the communists encourage the use of drugs. The communists of Red China are the world's leading exporters of opium, heroin, and similar hard drugs.

(2) MUSIC. There is also the communist encouragement of the wrong kind of music. Some young people sneer when others talk of the "wrong kind" of music. It is a fact, however, that the hypnotic music which is so commonly enjoyed by young people today actually results in lowered resistance to temptation and subversive ideas. Modern rock music features an overpowering beat which takes hold of the senses and the emotions. When that musical rhythm is accompanied, as it often is today, with subversive words, it is a potent weapon in the hands of the enemy. The former "High Priest" of LSD, Timothy Leary, agrees:

"The John Bircher who says rock 'n roll music encourages kids to take drugs is absolutely right. It's part of our plot. Drugs are the most efficient way to revolution," the lean graying Leary added. "The key to the future is the pleasure revolution we're experiencing today . . . and the lyrics and sound have the same effect as a drug—a jumbling of your reflex response."(*Berkeley Daily Gazette,* February 1, 1969.)

Art Linkletter, television personality, sorrowing after his daughter's suicide which was caused by use of LSD, said, "Record companies, disc jockeys and rock bands are controlled by the missionaries of this subculture." He estimated that at least half of the most popular teenage records of the day "are concerned with secret messages to teeners—drop out, turn on and groove with chemicals" (*The Register*).

Frequently the subversive words attached to these musical favorites exalt immorality, scoff at patriotism, advocate burning draft cards, and promote communist objectives.

(3) BLURRING OF THE SEXES. Another prevalent trend today is the blurring of the sexes, aimed at making boys look like girls, and girls like boys. The result is the encouragement of weakness at the time of budding young manhood and womanhood.

(4) ATTACK ON OUR INSTITUTIONS. If the communists are to make large numbers of our young people immoral, weak, confused, and ignorant, they will have to attack this nation's institutions. That means attacking or subverting the schools, the reading of good literature, the guidance of parents and the church. Communism is out to destroy or corrupt these institutions.

We must understand this communist program and help our young people to understand it. Communists are not, of course, at the bottom of everything that is troubling our young people today. Admittedly, some of the things which are the target of youth's revolt are undesirable. But we must not allow youth to be led into believing that the so-called "issues" are all valid issues. Many are mere pretexts. The real issue is the planned neutralization of the younger generation. This is accomplished by making young people immoral, weak, confused, and ignorant. *This* in turn is facilitated by keeping them immature.

HOW TO GET YOUNG PEOPLE
TO REMAIN IMMATURE

How would the communists get young people to fall for the very positions and activities that communists plan for them? Here the communist knowledge of psychology is profound. The whole communist conspiracy is based upon the knowledge of depth psychology. Communist psychologists, one can judge from the results, have concluded that if young people are to be useful to their program, they *must be kept immature.* This will harness the worst in them for the purposes the Party has in mind. They are not yet successful, but they are well on the way, and only when we and our young people understand their methods can we prevent them.

The Communist Party sets its goals far into the future. It has "five-year plans," "ten-year plans," not only for domestic production in the Soviet Union, but to achieve victory over enemies abroad. Communists work ceaselessly toward these long-range goals, and they are adept at using everything that occurs to their advantage. They take advantage of every trend that will weaken our youth into submission. But first they must be led down the path of immaturity.

Spoiled Children. The communists and their dupes and sympathizers, consciously or unconsciously, are working in harmony to encourage young people to act like immature, spoiled children.

If we were to describe childish behavior at its worst, we would say that the person who exhibits it is dirty, irresponsible, self-pitying, rude, destructive, contemptuous, and demanding rights without earning them. As a young person matures we have a right to expect that he will overcome these traits. If he, however, continues in this condition, he is not accepted by his parents, and, furthermore, society will not accept him. Unwillingness to accept or reward immaturity is the strongest force working upon young people to make them mature.

The communists know that there is a desire within all of us to remain children, and thus to be relieved of responsibility for our actions—demanding our rights instead of earning them. So, if *they* can provide a young person with a kind of acceptance from his own peer group (when because of immaturity he is rejected by parents and society) he will more readily remain in this condition. Increasingly youth groups are springing up which say, "We don't care if you are dirty, irresponsible, self-pitying, rude, destructive, contemptuous, and demanding rights without earning them. We accept you anyway." Hence, young people can remain childish and yet find acceptance.

The "immaturity cult" is permeating this nation's schools, where some teachers follow the plans for subversion unknowingly. Some urge students who are reaching an age of maturity to bring blankets and toys to school for cuddling. Others encourage high school students to use four letter words—any four letter words—in class. A professor in a large California State College (reports John W. Gilbaugh, Professor of Education, San Jose State College) admits that with his college students, he uses "Little Kid Talk in which I talk to the 'six-year-old' inside the 'adult' to help him get in touch with feelings."

The cult of immaturity seems to find adherents in the most unlikely—and unfortunate—places; for example, among those clothed in professorial, ministerial, and judicial robes. Much of the country was shocked a few years ago at an Associated Press photo of a gaunt old man in a black robe dancing in a church aisle with a teenage girl in shorts. He was a professor and clergyman at a southern university. This ludicrous antic was supposed to represent "a spontaneous rite of joy in worship." It succeeded in making an old man whose station and role would seem to presume some dignity look an utter fool, and in engendering so much protest that the university had to issue a public apology.

Another incredible example is more recent. Herbert Simms, Professor of Speech at Temple University, gave an address on "Communism and Social Change," which was printed in *Vital Speeches*, February 1, 1976, though I cannot imagine why anyone should think it vital in any respect. Part of it went as follows:

> I vividly recall one incident on a crowded beach at Big Sur in 1970. Early in the day a handful of young people had taken off their clothes and were frolicking in the sand. By 4 P.M. a large section of the beach had become a veritable nudist colony. Here were scores of ordinary middle-aged folk, bedecked in swimsuits by Jantzen and beach robes by Pucci who were suddenly confronted with the lifestyles of another

culture—and were liking it! Their exemplars were showing them more by deeds than by words that there was perhaps a better life to be lived; one of joy and liberation; a life in the now rather than in the future; an alternative to the controlled, humdrum existence that is the daily experience of most of us. Of course, these ordinary folk are back to work once again, and so, I presume, are the flower children who inspired them that day.

The professor is probably dead wrong on his last assumption. The flower children were not likely to go back to work like ordinary folk. No doubt they were frolicking in other places—flowered vans, communes, or other public areas; in abandoned houses or on the roadside. Do you feel "inspired" by adults who find life one big playground, with play, sex, drugs, and amusement the toys they have substituted for pacifiers, dolls, and kiddie cars?

The incredible and appalling factor, however, is not the behavior of young people like the capering nudists or the young woman dancing in the church aisle; it is the ridiculous, lugubrious, simpering approbation of older people—especially the clergy and the professors who should be examples of maturity and judgment to young people.

Happily, there are some exceptions. There was a case in which a high school counselor was talking to a group of parents about an eighteen-year-old boy who was causing so many problems in the school. "But," explained the counselor, "he had a terribly troubled childhood." "Well," came the rejoinder from one disgruntled parent, "why doesn't he consider growing up?"

WHY DO SO MANY YOUNG PEOPLE HATE?

A deeper study of the psychology of all this reveals that when young people behave in this (dirty, irresponsible, self-pitying, rude, destructive, contemptuous, demanding) manner they begin to despise *themselves*. Destructive self-hate is the result. But the ego cannot long stand self-hatred. Self-hatred leads to self-destructive behavior, and eventually, in some cases, to suicide. It is no wonder, then, that one of the highest causes of death among young people today in the college age group is suicide! They hate themselves, their looks, their minds, their own weaknesses; and they begin to feel unloved and misunderstood.

Of course, most young people will not take the extreme way out which leads to suicide. They will, instead, project their hatred outward upon other things: society, the nation, the church, God, logic, good taste, the establishment, the older generation, parents, pastors, and priests. All of these become the objects of their hatred. Thus, communists have found the secret of making those who have not matured go on a crusade of destruction against the symbols of maturity. By destroying good things, they gain some sense of satisfaction with their own behavior. They have a natural hostility for the superiority of adults, who have privileges, possessions, and seeming power that they may desire. What they cannot have, they destroy.

In the September 5, 1969, issue of *Time* magazine, a noted psychoanalyst, Bruno Bettelheim, comments on this fact:

> "The claim by radicals that they act out of high motives," Bettelheim believes, and "their occasional on target attack on real evils, have misled many well-meaning people into overlooking their true motive. This is hate, not a desire for a better world." . . . Dr. Bettelheim does not deny the existence of injustices within U.S. life. But he insists that the underlying causes of campus unrest lie as much in the way American children are raised and educated, as in the Vietnamese war or widespread poverty. His advice is for universities to act like firm but understanding parents.

In other words, the causes of much of the turmoil among youth is that many young people, rather than doing anything about their shortcomings, have become haters of themselves. But they are encouraged to continue *as they are* by those who profess to give them acceptance, and who urge them to project their hatred toward what they call "the establishment." Dr. Bettelheim goes on to say:

> In most of the small group of leaders of the radical left, intellect was developed at much too early an age, and at the

expense of their emotional development. Although exceedingly bright, some remained emotionally fixated at the age of the temper tantrum.

Discipline, order, and character, not permissiveness, are the foundation of learning. Even psychiatrists are recognizing the source of the problem. Young people have been kept immature, although they are assured that they are wise, and that the older generation should be learning from them and listening to them.

America is reaping the fruits of this harvest of permissiveness. John Dewey, the father of Progressive Education, visited Russia in the late 1920s and came away enamored of Soviet pragmatism. His widespread permissive ideas on education (*Impressions of Soviet Russia*) have been a potent factor in today's problems. He wanted individuals to be freed from competitive struggle, with guarantees of comfort, ease, and security. Under his influence, the status of perpetual infancy was taught as desirable by "progressive" educators. The fact that Soviet Russian educational systems follow no such theories of impotent anti-intellectualism escapes many. All of this, says Mortimer Smith, in his book entitled, *And Madly Teach*, "reduces education to a vast bubbling confusion. . . ."

The evolutionary hypothesis is another degrading factor in education which has aided the communists. Evolution in its purest form teaches that man does not have a soul, and without a soul he is only an animal on a higher level. Thus, if we behave like animals, who can be judgmental?

This is part of the result of the evolutionary theory being taught to replace the Judeo-Christian teaching of creation. Communism is based on evolution and teaches that man is not made by God, but is a product of nature, and has no immortal soul.

Materialistic evolutionism, or humanism, rejects any authority except that of each individual. R. J. Rushdoony writes:

> Because Humanism makes man his own authority, it enthrones childishness, self-indulgence, and tantrums, over maturity, self-disciplining and reason. Much of the [student and civil rights] protests have been marked by more emphasis on childishness than on issues. . . .
> This impulse is deeply imbedded in our humanistic age.

Not too long ago, a television interviewer asked a group of guests, kindergarten children all, what they would most like to be. The answers were the same: they all wanted to be babies! Why? Because, they answered, babies have nothing to do, and they are cared for! There was a time when kindergarten children wanted to be grown-ups; this was the social ideal, maturity. . . . Is it any wonder that authority is gone? A baby has to be trained into respect for authority, but grown-up babies are at war against authority, and therefore at war against life as God ordained it.

To sanction all-out permissive conduct will be to breed a generation of jaded misfits, unable to reach maturity. To teach young people that this life is all there is, that there is no soul, no God, no judgment, final regard, or final accounting is to make them totally wrapped up in the present. You will have robbed them of their hopes and ideals, and they can only become weak creatures immersed completely in the desire for material comfort and body experiences.

There is another contributing factor in today's slide toward degradation and that is what the Bible refers to as lust. Many of the behavior patterns today are simply a product of the encouragement of lust—lust for ease, lust for sex, lust for things that belong to others. Lust is a hybrid that produces envy, murder, and theft.

IS COMMUNISM REALLY THE CAUSE?

There is scarcely any doubt that communism, using its diabolic, sophisticated knowledge of depth psychology, and its long-range planning, is witnessing even unhoped for success as it has been targeting in on American youth. And unless we begin to understand these plans and the manipulation of our greatest asset—youth—the communists will very possibly succeed.

Behind communism stands Satan, who has found in it perhaps one of the strongest weapons that he has ever developed. We cannot account, otherwise, for the amazing results in the realm of evil that communism has achieved. Beyond any mere human level of endeavor, today's trends and practices are stained with supernatural evil. It is Satan who would destroy the faith, the hopes, and the youth of this nation that is the envy of every nation on earth.

WHAT IS THE CURE?

There are many remedies which might strengthen youth so that they could resist indoctrination and conditioning by subversives; but there is no guarantee that they could then resist the enemy. Some of the solutions are psychological, some sociological, some educational, and they might be temporarily helpful—*remedial* but not *curative*.

The cure, of course, is to convince people that God loves them. Then they cannot hate themselves, and they will not hate society. When you really believe that God loves you, you know that you are too precious in his sight to be wasted.

This is the task for all of us who have perceived the meaning of the forces influencing our young people today. We must help our young people; we must keep them from wasting themselves.

SEVEN CARDINAL RULES
OF TEACHING PATRIOTISM TO YOUNG PEOPLE

1. Set an early example of personal patriotism. Display the flag, discuss America's ideals, explain America's problems, vote, participate in public affairs with the young. Your example is your first and best teacher.

2. Teach reverence. Patriotism is one of the emotions and loyalties of reverence. Only when a child is taught reverence for God, the sacredness of life, and the rights of others, can he learn patriotism.

3. Keep the child from the influence of corrupters. We learn values by learning what to avoid as well as what to embrace. Movies, television, books, companions that scoff at patriotism or exalt the enemies of America should be off limits and the reasons explained.

4. Discuss school work with young people. If you find un-American ideas, point them out. Even if you have to protest to the school authorities, do so. Let no unpatriotic idea or teaching go unchallenged.

5. Be sure of your facts. Responsibility in teaching the young begins with a reasonable, factual approach. If the young person can catch you in an error of fact or an unreasonable opinion he will reject everything else you say.

6. Raise your children in a church which stands for patriotism. The church should teach the highest values. If it is unpatriotic or obviously opposed to freedom by its advocacy of socialism or the appeasement of communism, *change churches.* Don't be a spiritual dropout, but find or start a church which preaches the gospel, affirms patriotism, and opposes socialism and communism.

7. Choose colleges carefully. The wrong college (there are many) can undo in a year what you have done for a lifetime. The right college (they are few) may be less convenient or less desirable in some unimportant ways. Put first things first. Colleges are often life destroyers. Do not *send* a young person to college, help him *help himself.*

Totally subsidized education leads to the notion of socialism, and allows much idle time for the wrong kind of social life, and for participation in unwholesome student activity.

One of the bywords of communists is "equality." There is a continual cry that all men are equal and therefore must receive equal treatment. This is nonsense. It is true, as the Declaration of Independence says, that "all men are *created* equal." They do not *stay* equal. Were Abraham Lincoln and Al Capone equals? Douglas MacArthur and John Dillinger? George Washington and Benedict Arnold?

There is another terrible misconception that young people should get straight. The Constitution guarantees the right to the *pursuit* of happiness. It does *not* guarantee that happiness will be handed to every citizen on a silver platter.

We have had in recent years a runaway buildup of impossible expectations. People have been led to believe that they are entitled to be supported with no effort on their part. We have been led to believe that by busing and mixing all children together, they will all receive an equal education. They will not. We have been led to believe that with minimum wages, shorter working hours, pensions, hospitalization insurance, Social Security, and other benefits, workers will be happy, productive, and loyal. Not all of them are.

Sex, drugs, unrestricted leisure, marching, protesting, communal living, and studied nonconformity have not made many young people happy. They will become happy when they find things *worth* believing in and living for—God, home, family, duty, and country.

SIX
TEACH
YOUR CHILD
SELF-RELIANCE

When we hear a certain word or phrase again and again, the meaning tends to be lost, and our consciousness simply registers certain sounds. Periodically we should stop and consider the true implications of words we hear or use often—words like love, duty, responsibility, patriotism, maturity, and *free enterprise.*

In this context, the word "free" certainly does not imply that enterprise has no cost; far from it. It is intended to mean that enterprise should be exercised with a minimum of curtailment or restraint and a maximum of freedom. Unhappily, the trend is just the opposite; enterprise is becoming less and less free, more and more encumbered and restricted.

But what is "enterprise"? According to the dictionary, it is "an undertaking which involves activity, courage, energy; an important or daring project," and "the character or disposition that leads one to attempt the difficult, the untried."

Enterprise need not refer only to business. Those who explored the new world and established trade routes or missions, were men of rare enterprise. The men who built canals and railroads were entrepreneurs, but perhaps not so brave as the thousands of others who put their families and possessions into creaking wagons and set off across the mountains to begin a new life and build a new nation.

Enterprise is indeed daring, and implies vision and a bold spirit, whether it finds its outlet in commerce and trade, in voyaging and exploration, in art or science, in education, government, or even in religion.

Enterprise, of course, may work good or evil. Napoleon was a man of boundless enterprise, but his life brought bloodshed and devastation to Europe, and there have never been more enterprising men in producing a holocaust of evil than Lenin and those who have followed him.

In all times and in all lands, there have been enterprising men, but probably never as many who have built so much in so short a time as in this great and blessed country. Yet, unfortunately, how few of our young people know and appreciate our history.

They will certainly not hear it from many of our politicians, even though they are themselves the beneficiaries of the free enterprise system. They will not hear it from the media, whose life blood is the advertising revenues contributed by business. And they will certainly not hear it from teachers and professors in the classrooms, where a deep-seated hostility to business seems to be a credential for a teaching certificate.

Thank goodness, then, for one educator who had something refreshingly frank and different to say on this subject. Typically, he represents one of the small colleges. He is Dr. Milton Upton, President, Beloit College, Beloit, Wisconsin. He said this:

> I have just about reached the end of my tolerance for the way our society seems to have sympathy only for the misfit, the pervert, the drug addict, the ne'er-do-well, the maladjusted, the chronic criminal, the under-achiever, the loser—in general—the underdog.
>
> I feel it is time for someone like me to stand up and say: "I'm for the upperdog." I'm for the achiever—the one who sets out to do something and does it; the one who recognizes the problems and opportunities at hand and endeavors to deal with them; the one who is successful at his immediate task because he is not worrying about someone else's failings; the one who doesn't consider it "square" to be constantly looking for something more to do, and who isn't always rationalizing why he shouldn't be doing what he is doing; the one, in short, who carries the work of his part of the world squarely on his shoulders.
>
> We are born equal in rights but not in talent, and the more

talented are no more responsible for their talents than the underprivileged for their plight. The measure of each should be by what he does with his inherited position.

We will never create a good society—much less a great one—until individual excellence and achievement is not only respected but encouraged. That is why I'm for the upperdog—the achiever—the succeeder.

And another very wise man, Eric Hoffer, made this profoundly true observation:

We cannot win the weak by sharing our wealth with them, nor by sharing our hope, pride, or even hatred. Our healing gift to the weak is the capacity for self-help.

Small wonder that a business executive spoke up angrily at a stockholders' meeting and said:

Are we lepers? Are we criminals? Are we outcasts? Where are our Oscars? Where are our Emmys? Where are our medals and citations for minding the store, for keeping the wheels turning, the engines running, and doing business as usual while the reformers, the protesters, the malcontents, the consumerists, the do-gooders are demonstrating, marching, picketing, shouting, preaching, lobbying and propagandizing—and always within range of the microphones, the cameras, and the newspaper reporters?

But who keeps TV and radio on the air so that its newscasters and commentators can denigrate and excoriate business, and its comics and entertainers can ridicule and lampoon business? Why, business, of course. . . .

You hear pleas every day for good causes—the cancer fund, heart fund, cerebral palsy, muscular dystrophy, mental illness, etc. They are fine. But you hear about them from singers and performers and show business or sports people. In your community who heads the drives, organizes the campaigns, does the leg work and brings in the money? It's the business men, isn't it? Fine. We don't complain. But even if we don't get any credit, at least, shouldn't the knocking, and mudslinging, and dirty tricks stop for awhile?

Of course they should. But they don't seem to. The same story was told recently by one of the *Wall Street Journal's* very able and reliable columnists in an article titled: "Take Off the Gloves." Mr. Raymond K. Price has this to say:

> In recent years there has been an avalanche of antibusiness demagoguery, not only from populist politicians and their labor leader allies, but also from professional consumerists and their academic acolytes. A whole generation has been raised to regard business as, at best, a necessary evil, and at worst, a corrupt predator. A suspicious, cynical political atmosphere has been created in which the office-holder who rises in defense of business interests does so at the risk of his political neck. The essential nexus between the health of the goose and the supply of golden eggs has been all but lost.
>
> The appalling economic ignorance of the American public was pointed up in a recent poll which shows that Americans think that corporate profits amount to 28% of sales. At a time when high prices are viewed as public enemy No. 1, this is precisely the sort of gross misconception that feeds a destructive climate in which the free enterprise system is increasingly threatened by punitive political measures.
>
> The American public desperately needs an education, not only in figures, but also in the way business operates; the obstacles it has to overcome, the role of incentives, the means of capital accumulation, the costs of technology. And it needs executives with fire in their bellies and the facts in their heads to conduct this education. Maybe the American free enterprise system will come up with an effective army of defenders before it's too late.

Perhaps so—but the signs are distressingly lacking. And in the meantime the detractors of business grow ever more numerous and noisy.

It is man's destiny to be enterprising, to work, and to be productive. The Scriptures admonish us:

> If any would not work, neither should he eat. For we hear that there are some which walk among you disorderly, working not at all, but are busybodies. Now them that are

such we command and exhort with quietness they work and eat their own bread (2 Thessalonians 3:11).

Many other wise and good men have said so:

Overworking others is wrong. Underworking yourself is a sin.   —Herbert Hoover

Work is a divine gift. Man's highest blessedness is that he toil and know wherefore he toils.   —Nathaniel Hawthorne

The sum of wisdom is that, that time is never lost which is devoted to work.   —Ralph Waldo Emerson

It is one of the tragedies of our time—and one that will become more and more evident in the future—that so many of our young people are "turned off" by business. Even in a time of high unemployment, business must send recruiters by the thousands to college campuses to scout for talent, while young people turn more readily to what they deem the "creative" or "humanitarian" areas: sociology, counseling, social work, the Peace Corps, consumerism, ecology, and the like.

And yet who is the most creative man in our society? Isn't it the job creator? Isn't it the businessman who not only risks his own capital, his own future, his credit and reputation in his enterprise, but creates the opportunity for others to make a livelihood?

Without the entrepreneurs in our society who (despite the crushing weight of taxation for government spending programs, despite the suffocating pressures of bureaucracy) continue to create jobs, our economy surely would have collapsed. And yet we hear a rising crescendo of demands for billions for "government created jobs." We hear proposals for "government guaranteed jobs," which simply means that any person who says he cannot find a job (perhaps because he is lazy, incompetent, unreliable, or worse) will be assigned a job by the government, or if it has none, will be given a living wage as a dole. If, God forbid, such a law should be enacted, it would be likely to create five or ten million jobs overnight.

If there is anything approaching a miracle in our society today, it is that the spirit of enterprise has survived the concerted assaults against it from all sides—assaults which have mounted in fury since 1932 and the advent of the New Deal, with all of its repressive antibusiness legislation. It is proof indeed that the passion of man to work for his own dream, his ambition to excel, his wish to dare, to compete, to sink or swim on his own is unquenchable. It is the same spirit that drove men to sail the oceans, even when they did not know what lay beyond the horizons (perhaps monsters and death); which drives men to climb the highest mountains, to explore the bottom of the sea, to reach the moon, and to plan for the ultimate conquest of space. It is in the nature of some men to pit themselves against the most severe, seemingly insuperable obstacles and odds.

Now, of course, the one absolutely indispensable factor in teaching your child about free enterprise is that *you* believe in it yourself; that you believe it is the force and the system which built up America and made it great.

One man who is a strong believer in free enterprise and the American way is a man known essentially as a humorist, Sam Levenson. Mr. Levenson, like another great American humorist, Will Rogers, is an eloquent advocate of free enterprise. Both had the good fortune to be born into families in which income was low but family feeling, standards, and ambitions were high. Both became famous and successful, but also highly respected and much loved, because they were human beings of great warmth, great integrity, and great spirituality. They believed in God, in family, in America, and in all of the principles and institutions that made America great and created the opportunities for their own greatness.

Sam Levenson, who has written a wonderful book: *In One Era and Out the Other,* explains the title this way:

> I started out in one era and arrived in another. The trip took half a lifetime. By the time I got to my good old dream castle at the end of the rainbow, it had been condemned and replaced by something more up-to-date in prefabricated temporary contemporary. I'm not sure whether I got here too late for the old world or too soon for the new one. I am hung up between two eras. My hair is getting gray, some of it from aging, some of it from the falling plaster of venerable institutions crumbling over my head.

There is much truth in what he says. Some of that falling plaster is from the institution of free enterprise. And that institution was made up of the traits of thrift, frugality, hard work, self-discipline, risk taking, and resourcefulness.

Some of that plaster may also be from the venerable institutions of marriage and the family, of which Mr. Levenson speaks with great feeling and force in his book. He stresses a great one-liner his father was fond of repeating to his children:

> If you ever need a helping hand, you always know where to find it—right there at the end of your arm.

One may wonder what would be the reaction of some young persons today to such an admonition from a parent. For along with the flowers and beads and marijuana and rock music, there has grown a cult of dependency among many young people. For all their protests against the hypocrisy and shallowness of society, they have been more than willing for society to make provision for them, in the form of student loans, various government grants, food stamps, and miscellaneous handouts.

Levenson's book points out the dramatic contrast between the old-fashioned self-reliance of his generation and the supine and spineless attitude of those today who want federal room service, and federal house calls for the slightest problem or inconvenience. It is a degrading and shameful attitude and one from which we must protect our young people at all cost.

SEVEN
THE CHRISTIAN
EDUCATION
OF YOUR CHILD

Train up a child in the way he should go: and when he is old, he will not depart from it (Prov. 22:6).

But Jesus said, Suffer little children, and forbid them not, to come unto me: for of such is the kingdom of heaven (Matt. 19:14).

Go ye therefore and teach all nations, baptizing them in the name of the Father, and of the Son, and of the Holy Ghost: Teaching them to observe all things whatsoever I have commanded you (Matt. 28:19, 20).

Christianity is a teaching and an evangelizing faith. Christ commissioned his disciples and sent them into a pagan and hostile world, charged to teach men the truth. Unhappily, in many churches, this teaching fervor has subsided and they have turned instead to social and racial reforms. But like charity, Christian teaching begins at home, with one's own children, as God instructed from the beginning.

Not since the earliest days of Christianity, when the disciples walked dusty, weary roads and endured every manner of abuse and ill treatment and sacrifice, has the Christian faced such a hostile, materialistic, cynical, and secular world as today. Atheistic communism continues to spread its suffocating mantle over millions. Various forms of socialist and leftist ideologies, all repressive, most bitterly antireligious, extend their influence into government, into schools, into the media, and even into the churches.

Tragically, this is the case right here in our own country. This poisonous infusion and infiltration is succeeding because of the indifference of many people, so that we are in peril of losing our most precious possession—our young people.

Many parents today seem willing to sacrifice their own offspring through apathy, neglect, and self-indulgence. Igor Kon, a Soviet sociologist writing in *Soviet Life* (Sept., 1975), in an article, "The Generation Old and New," points out that the influence of parents over children is declining rapidly even in the Soviet Union. He observes:

> An important psychological factor in the world of the teenager is the coeval society: classmates, mass organizations (Young Pioneers, Young Communist League) sports clubs, informal groups and unions. Studies show that people of their own age have the greatest influence on the young. Not least in importance, the mass media has made the young much more independent of their elders.

In the sixties many young people blindly followed radical "leaders," accepting their standards of dress, speech, conduct, morals, and life style almost without question. Young people still tend to "follow the leader" in their attitudes on sex, marijuana, general decorum, parental discipline or guidance, choosing a career, etc. They are also strongly influenced by the media—particularly television and motion pictures—which present an immoral life as socially acceptable and even desirable. Most parents and children today do not spend as much time in the home or with the family as they did a generation or two ago. These are facts.

These adverse factors are part of the climate in which the parents must consider their teaching responsibilities. Parents are obligated by the laws of God and of the State to see to it that their children are properly educated. But the State is continually encroaching upon the rights and responsibilities of the parents and is attempting to dictate what the child shall be taught, and how and where. Those parents who believe strongly that education must include teaching about God and his laws are increasingly feeling the hostility of secular authority.

In Bradford, Ohio, a number of parents joined together to found the Tabernacle Christian School. A very basic, strong educational curriculum was adopted, but there was also heavy emphasis on religious and moral principles. Then the State educational authorities investigated the school and arbitrarily determined that it did not conform to the minimum standards prescribed by the Board of Education—which consisted of more than 500 different regulations and requirements. The administrator of the school, Levi W. Whisner, contended that not a single school in the state could conform completely to all of these regulations.

The parents refused to remove their children from the Tabernacle Christian School and send them to public schools; whereupon a suit was brought by the State to compel them to do so. Two-thirds of the sixty-five students enrolled in the school came from families which were not members of the Tabernacle School. Their parents simply felt that they would receive a better education at this Christian school than at the Bradford public schools. Tabernacle students attend chapel service once a week, memorize a chapter of the Bible each month, and have worship every day.

Stanford Achievement Tests taken by these children showed that they scored higher in basic skills than public school children. The attorney representing the school, William Ball, said:

> There is a place in our society for small schools. The children in Tabernacle Christian School are being raised as good moral citizens. Ohio education authorities are trying to compel independent schools to fit the public school mold. If a religious school must be a carbon copy of the public school, what reason does it have to exist?

The parents and authorities of the Tabernacle Christian School made the following objections to sending their children to public schools:

> 1. The Board of Education allocated all instructional time in the schools, with no allowance for Bible or religious instruction, thus preventing the Bible from being the central factor in education, as it should be.

2. The regulation that: "All activities shall conform to policies adopted by the Board of Education" is simply a blank check for the State to run the school and exclude God.

3. Board of Education rules refused access of parents to school records pertaining to their children—this is contrary to God's law and the rights and responsibilities of parents in rearing their children.

4. The public school's method of solving problems by the consensus of students takes no account of God or morality.

5. Social studies prescribed by the State take no account of God or the moral code, or of the soul.

6. Studies prescribed by the Board of Education teach that moral standards constantly change—of course, they do not.

In a similar case, also in Ohio, the state sued three sets of parents for child neglect for sending their children to the Winchester Christian Academy. Imagine being sued for *child neglect* for providing your children with a Christian education! This case demonstrates the lengths to which secular authorities will go to take control of children.

The Winchester School had a curriculum similar to that of the Tabernacle Christian School; it was a Bible-oriented program of education in basic subject areas, promoting self-reliance, with highly individualized instruction called Accelerated Christian Education.

The suit could have made the children wards of the State, but it was dropped one day before trial when the lawyer for the parents demanded proof that *every* public school was being operated in full compliance with Board of Education standards, and demanded records of all schools in the district and records of inspection of all schools. So in this case the Christian parents prevailed, but this certainly does not mean the end of efforts and schemes of secular authorities to get control of our children—using the full power of the State to do so.

Another application of this attitude is seen in all of the attempted solutions to the problems of minorities: a search for answers in all the wrong places—schools, busing, new types of tests and grading systems, changed curricula, so-called "affirmative action" in schools, business, and government, special grants, welfare, and other government programs. None of these proposed solutions have worked well nor will they work well, because the only right solution is through the family. The family is one rock for stability, for effective moral teaching and true "life adjustment," which must mean adjustment to God's will and his Word. The church is—or should be—the other rock of spiritual stability.

A strong protest toward this creeping secularization of education came recently, as one would expect, from the Catholic Church, which has seen the numbers and influence of its schools constantly diminish in recent years. An editorial in *Columbia*, April, 1976, reads:

> The increasingly secular culture being fostered in America by liberal media, government agencies, and particularly by judicial decrees, is forcing the very opposite values (from Catholic parents) on national life. "No fault" divorce laws assume that marriage is a temporary response to human instincts, and that it buds, blooms, and dies like the flowers relegated to the compost heap in the fall. A pleasure-oriented view of life spread by the media and reinforced by the courts reduces sex to an object of enjoyment. Sex has become a part of the American throw-away culture whose byword is: "Use and Discard."
>
> The importance of man's relationship to God is ignored, downgraded, and even scoffed at in many segments of American society. Religion is deigned only minuscule attention in the public media. Even then it is often given notice only as a source of novelty or ridicule.
>
> In a sharp break with early American tradition, the courts have decreed that prayer and religion cannot be introduced as voluntary formative elements in the education of children in public schools.

The *Columbia* editorial makes many sound points, including the final one. It is very true that the early American tradition placed great emphasis on God and the church and the family: Catholics in Maryland, Quakers in Pennsylvania, Episcopalians in Virginia, Puritans in New England. And now, while children may not pray in school, they are becoming a prey to the constant, ruthless design of the communist-socialist-leftist bloc. This bloc seeks to destroy the family and assume control of children.

There is, apparently, a movement on foot to introduce "moral education" into the public schools, but it is moral education in the form of a poll; i.e., one in which students discuss an ethical problem, and then resolve it by a consensus vote! So stealing or cheating or sexual aberrations might be agreed upon as proper and permissible, "depending on the circumstances."

There is a commentary on this development in *McCalls*, March, 1976, by Kenneth Woodward, in an article, "Who Should Teach Your Children Right from Wrong?" Mr. Woodward tells of observing, with other parents, seventh grade students discussing a "moral dilemma" in which a student is presumed to find a football which he knows has been stolen by another student. Shall he keep it, give it to the thief, return it to the owner, or simply leave it where it is? There was a long discussion and many comments, but the problem was left unresolved by the students—a fact which is ominous, because, obviously, there is only one clear and proper choice. Mr. Woodward makes this observation:

> I was troubled. This was the sort of moral examination, I felt, that parents should conduct at home. "You may be right," the teacher allowed, "but the parents of most children I work with would never bother."
>
> Like most parents, I was completely unaware that in schools all across the United States—public as well as private—officials are adding classes in moral education. In New York, for instance, the Department of Education estimates that 80% of the State's primary and secondary schools offer some kind of program designed to help students clarify their values and measure their conduct.

Liberals do not like the words *moral* or *morals*. Instead, they substitute the word *values*, which, of course, is not at all the same. Mr. Woodward continues:

> The major reason (for such "moral education" programs) say proponents, is that the school must fill the vacuum left by the declining moral influence of the parents and religious

institutions. And a majority of American parents apparently agree. In its latest annual survey of public attitudes toward education, the Gallup Poll reports 72% of Americans favor (with 15% opposed) instruction in the schools that would deal with morals and moral behavior.

Of course, the argument that there is a "vacuum" into which government must step is an old liberal ploy. This was always the argument by which government intrusion into business was justified, until today it is stifling and smothering its victim—and the end is not in sight. The same argument was used to begin the federalizing of education, and this takeover is proceeding with alarming acceleration.

It is unhappily true that many parents have been delinquent in moral instruction, and also true that many churches—led by the National Council of Churches—have virtually abandoned the traditional role of the church in nurturing its young. But this certainly does not mean that this God-given function should pass by default to the government—regardless of what Gallup polls may indicate. Mr. Woodward concludes with a sound admonition:

> Despite these arguments, conscientious parents ought to be wary of relinquishing moral education to teachers and school psychologists. A generation ago psychiatrists like Dr. Benjamin Spock encouraged parents to rely on child-care experts in raising their children. Today Dr. Spock warns that the net effect of much expert psychological advice "has been to make many doubt their own standards and to dilute them—quite drastically—as they have passed them on to their children."

We have mentioned only some of the very real dangers that confront Christian parents in a secular world. Unless you are unusually fortunate, it is not likely that you live in a community where there is a strong, vital Christian solidarity, such as existed, for example, in many of the early villages and settlements in this country two hundred years ago and more. But this type of community is what we must seek to build.

enough to understand the moral and spiritual implication of what he is doing.

Parents often allow children to be received into the church and baptized when they do not, in fact, know whether the child is spiritually prepared. Many Christians do not believe in infant baptism; that is, the baptism of babies. But have you stopped to think that there is really *no difference* in baptizing a baby who is too young to believe for himself, and a ten-year-old child—if the ten-year-old does not know what he is doing?

In both cases we are baptizing people who are not believers and *this is infant baptism* regardless of the difference in ages. Therefore, it follows that, to be a real Christian, a child must be *old enough to be a believer.*

How much must a child comprehend of the teachings of Christianity before he can be truly saved? A child does not need to understand all of the doctrines of Christianity before he can be saved. But there are some which he *must* understand before he can intelligently believe.

Some parents feel that if the child is old enough to "love" Jesus, then he is old enough to be saved. This is, of course, erroneous. It may sound attractive, but let us analyze it. To "love" Jesus is a very serious thing. It is not the same kind of love that a child bestows upon a favorite toy or upon a companion with whom he plays. Love for Jesus is a deep devotion to Christ. It is a glad surrender and a ready obedience to his will. Does the child who "loves" Jesus really understand what loving Jesus is? Does the child comprehend what it means to accept Jesus Christ as *Lord* as well as *Savior?*

Equally as important, does he understand who this one we call "Jesus" really is? I have found to my great surprise that we cannot take for granted that children understand who Jesus is. From earliest infancy they hear his name associated with lambs and flowers and entertaining little Bible stories. This is as it should be, for we must present Christ first on the level of a little child's understanding. But for Christ to be real enough to a child, so that the child may come into a personal relationship to him, means that the child is going to have to understand something about who Jesus is and what he has done.

One of the greatest dangers in speaking to children about their salvation is our careless habit of taking for granted that they understand the meaning of terms. Children are ready to copy the sayings and phrases of others. Very glibly they say, "I want to give my heart to Jesus" or "I want Jesus to come into my heart." But do they really understand what this means? One cannot be satisfied when a child gives this answer. One must probe deeper to find out if the child is merely using words which have no real meaning to him or if he really understands what he is saying.

Therefore, I suggest the following basic teachings about Christianity as necessary for a child to understand:

1. What sin is. Sin is the willful violation of the law and will of God. It is more than just telling lies or being naughty. It is the transgression of the will of God.

2. A personal consciousness of having sinned. A person cannot be saved from sin unless he recognizes that he *has* sinned. Children must be brought to see that sin is a moral choice which involves rebellion against the will of God as clearly revealed in the Bible.

3. A knowledge of the relationship between Jesus Christ and God the Father. A child need not understand all of the implications of the divine Trinity—Father, Son, and Holy Ghost—but he must know clearly the difference between God the Father and God the Son to see that God, *for Christ's sake,* forgives our sins and makes us children of God. Children are often taught to pray to Jesus in such a way as to give them the impression that *Jesus and God the Father* are the same. They can never understand God's fatherhood unless they understand that Jesus wins our forgiveness from his Heavenly Father by becoming our mediator. Prayer should be offered to God the Father in the name of Jesus, that is, in the merits or claims of Jesus upon his Father.

4. The simple meaning of Christ's death upon the cross. Children can easily be taught that someone must pay for our sins. Christ died for our sins on the cross, and we are forgiven because of his sacrifice on our behalf. This can be understood by a child.

5. The resurrection of Jesus Christ. Children must be taught that Christ is a person who lived not only in the past. They must understand that he is alive today. He can save here and now. After we become children of God he can answer our prayers. They must understand his *living presence* and his *intercession* on behalf of the believer. A child should have no trouble understandin the meaning of Easter.

6. The meaning of baptism. It is easy for a child to grasp the meaning of this important doctrine. If he accepts Christ, he will within a few days be asked to be baptized. He should be taught the meaning of baptism, so that when he is baptized he may enter entirely into an understanding of its significance. Baptism is, of course, a picture or drama enacting the fact of the believer's faith in the death, burial, and resurrection of Christ. We go down into the water to show that Jesus was buried. We come up out of the water to show that Jesus was raised from the dead for us.

7. The acceptance of Jesus Christ as Savior and Lord is a lifetime decision. Here is where so many fail to lead a child correctly. A child tends to live in the present, but he must be made to understand that when he becomes a Christian, he is surrendering his *entire life* to Jesus Christ. To be sure, a child cannot fully understand all that this involves. Nevertheless, he must realize that he is deciding that Jesus Christ will have full control of his life for as long as he lives.

Parents who are truly burdened about their children's salvation will so train them that early in life they may come to understand these simple doctrines. But these truths will not be absorbed by the child without a conscious effort by a parent, Sunday school teacher, or pastor. When a child understands these doctrines it will be easy to lead him to Christ. Without such knowledge it is hard, if not impossible, to do so.

We cannot expect our children to become born-again Christians without our thought, planning, and action.

QUESTION: *How can you tell when the child is ready to come to Christ and join the church?*

ANSWER: The child should exhibit the following signs:

1. He should become concerned about the effect of his sins upon his relationship to God.

2. He should be in love with the church and anxious to become a part of its fellowship.

3. He should exhibit evidence that he has a knowledge of the

difference between joining the church and becoming a born-again Christian.

When these three signs coincide, the child is ready to come to Christ and make a public profession of his faith in Christ as Savior and Lord.

QUESTION: *What is the responsibility of the parents in the salvation of the child?*

ANSWER: To train the child adequately in the vocabulary and doctrines of salvation, and in the meaning of church membership. This, of course, requires that the parents themselves have clear conceptions of these matters.

The parents should never press the child to come forward and accept Christ. There is danger that the child might do it only to please the parents. The child should come forward in a church service and make a public profession of faith in Christ *only when he chooses to do so.* God has left us free, and we must not coerce anyone else, especially our children.

Most parents who come regularly to church and bring their children do not have a problem in persuading their children to accept Christ. The child usually *wants* to join the church before he is truly under conviction for his sins. If the readiness of the mind and heart of the child coincides with previous instruction on the part of the parent, then the child will make his profession in the full knowledge of what he is doing and will be truly saved.

There are false signs which occasionally are seen and which sometimes make a parent wonder if the child is ready to be saved. Among these signs which should be examined carefully is the child's desire to become a member of the church because an older child, or a friend, has made a profession of faith.

Another is the desire to join the church because it seems that many people are doing it. A child is easily swayed and suggestible. We must guard him from his own immature emotions. Of course, there is danger in so discouraging him from the acceptance of Christ when God has convicted him of his need of the Savior. Nevertheless, this is not as great a danger as some suppose, because if a parent has been faithful in home training there will be very little doubt about the genuineness of the child's desire.

Another great danger in leading a child to Christ is the inclination to be *shallow* in dealing with the child. We must beware of not going deep enough. A halfway salvation is no salvation at all.

What a tragedy that a child should join the church without being truly born again, and for years go on in church membership, never realizing that he is *not* a child of God.

If the parent lacks the skill to deal with the child in this matter, he should seek the help of the pastor who, tactfully and yet earnestly, will assist either in instructing or probing to find whether the child is ready for salvation.

The finest way in which your pastor can serve you is to help ascertain whether or not your child is truly born again. A pastor who takes his work seriously will deal seriously with a child, even at the risk of offending the parents. Parents who become offended at a pastor's concern for the souls of their children are like the parent who resents a doctor's care over the child's physical well-being.

QUESTION: *What is the responsibility of the church in the salvation of the child?*

ANSWER: The church should provide Sunday school, training courses, teachers, and programs which present the way of salvation plainly to the pupil. Trained church leaders should seize every opportunity to make the way of salvation plain and to instruct children (from their late primary years especially through the junior years) in the areas of doctrine mentioned above. Programs should be so brought to the children's minds and hearts as to help them understand the way of salvation and motivate them toward accepting Christ.

The preaching services of the church should not be over the children's heads as far as Christian doctrines are concerned. To be sure, not every sermon can be on the level of childhood's understanding, but there should be elements in every sermon that children *can* understand.

Vacation Bible schools should be centered around presenting the way of salvation and the claims of Christ.

The young people's work of the church should influence through associations, fellowship, youth retreats, parties, and socials, as well as programs of inspiration.

The parents must, of course, assume their responsibility to bring the child to the church, so that the church may have the opportunity of living up to *its* responsibility.

If a parent really wants to be sure that his child is born again, let him bring him constantly to the evangelistic services of the church.

It is in the preaching of the gospel, through the evangelistic presentation of Christ to unbelievers, that children gradually come to know that they are sinners and how they can be saved.

Even after a child has made a profession of faith, it is important to keep him constantly under the influence of evangelism. Only through evangelism will he be kept from backsliding. Only through evangelism will he have the opportunity to make the many rededications that growing up in Christ requires. This is the parents' continuing responsibility.

What if the Sunday school teacher, the church, the parent or the pastor should make an error in leading a small child to Christ? If the parent is faithful in keeping the child under the influence of evangelism, sooner or later the Holy Spirit will have another opportunity to do his work firmly, deeply, and well.

A parent cannot sit back with a sigh of relief when his child becomes a Christian. The job is only partly finished. After conversion comes the long period of instruction in the real meaning of Christianity.

In today's world, the family, the basic unit of society, is under increasing attack. Materialism seeks to replace God as the center of the family, as parents try to give their children every material advantage possible. In addition, most American communities have an endless number of projects—many of them worthwhile, but which take a great deal of time and effort. All too often, little time is left to satisfy the spiritual life of the children. Nor can the fullness of life be achieved by a preoccupation with accumulating material possessions. Certainly the home should be as beautiful and as attractive as possible, but it is essential to remember that provision must also be made for children to grow in the knowledge and love of God in the home. The Sunday school cannot carry the burden of Christian training alone; the home must supplement and often anticipate the work of the Sunday school.

Teaching a child about God is not as difficult a task as many parents believe it to be. There is no substitute for this early experience of learning from father and mother about the love of God for his creatures, and his protection over their lives. Children are quick to recognize the vitality of their parents' commitment to their faith. Especially among older children, the depth of that commitment will be reflected in the child's devotion to God. Children who are fortunate enough to grow up in a family where

Christ is known, loved, and served will come to know about God through their parents, even before they are old enough to fully understand all the beliefs their parents hold.

Family life offers an excellent opportunity for teaching, especially Christian education. It is essential to take the child to Sunday school and church services, but the trust and love which a Christ-centered family displays toward God provide a natural setting for spiritual learning. A child begins to understand about love and trust through intimate association with the members of the family, and it is easy to use these evidences as a basis to teach him about God's love for him.

FAMILY DEVOTIONS

Nothing is more important as an aid to developing children's Christian character than regular family devotions. This period of time at the "family altar" provides the ideal opportunity for children to grow in the knowledge of the Lord. Even the smallest children, if they are old enough to talk, can be encouraged to take part in devotions, and often they enjoy having a part in family worship. The Bible admonishes parents to teach the Word of God "diligently unto thy children" (Deut. 6:7), and there is no better time to do this than when the family is gathered in warm, intimate fellowship, worshiping God together. Christian character cannot help but develop in such surroundings. The minds of children are deeply impressionable and the memories of such experiences leave their mark.

It is not possible to suggest a program for family devotions in great detail that will suit each family. Singing the great old hymns is often an effective way to give the children a firm foundation for their faith. They may not be able to understand every word they are singing, but in later years, perhaps in time of trouble, these hymns will be recalled and can give comfort or guidance. Also make use of the many excellent modern songs written especially for children.

The worship period will naturally include the reading of the Bible. Various methods may be used in selection of passages to be read. Many excellent books, such as devotional and Bible story books, may be used to good advantage as explanatory or supplemental reading. Children should be encouraged to memorize passages of Scripture which they can understand, and it should be impressed upon them that in time of need—no matter how small the need—these passages will be of great help. Religious bookstores offer many helpful aids such as contemporary translations of the Bible and Scripture memory cards.

A very important time of the family worship is prayer time. Children should be encouraged to offer their own prayers—those of thanks as well as of petition. Teach them that God is not to be regarded as a Santa Claus who will grant their every request. Children especially need to be reminded to give "thanks always for all things unto God and the Father in the name of our Lord Jesus Christ" (Eph. 5:20). Thus prayer can become a natural, normal part of their lives.

Children should be taught to pray *in the name of Jesus.* The New Testament is very clear in this teaching. In John 14:13, Jesus, in speaking to his disciples on the occasion of the Last Supper, said: "And whatsoever ye shall ask *in my name,* that will I do, that the Father may be glorified in the Son." Again, in John 15:16: ". . . that whatsoever ye shall ask of the Father *in my name,* he may give it you." There are many other references, but one final one will suffice. John 16:24: "Hitherto have ye asked nothing *in my name:* ask, and ye shall receive, that your joy may be full." Praying in Jesus' name is not an empty phrase. It means to offer prayer in the merits of the Savior rather than because of our own merits.

Prayers need not be long, for short prayers will encourage the younger children to take part. Prayer should become a vital part of family life. The intimacy of family devotions provides an ideal atmosphere for little misunderstandings to be righted. Instances of answered prayer can be related and thanks given to God for his goodness.

As children grow older, they will begin to ask questions concerning God. A common one is, "Why can't I see God?" It is not necessary to go into great detail in answering this question, but just to explain that God does not permit man to see him so that we may believe him through *faith.* If we could *see* him and *touch* him there would be no need for faith. Children should be reminded that we cannot *see* electricity, but we have faith to believe that when we press a switch the light will glow. When we come to God in faith and in prayer, the light of his presence will glow in our lives. Children do not seem to be particularly bothered by the fact that God will always be a presence in their lives, though not visible. If the father and mother accept the fact of God being invisible, but ever near, the children grow naturally into a love and an acceptance of God's nature too.

Another question that children frequently ask is, "Where is God?" This question can be answered by pointing out that God is everywhere, but his central dwelling place is in heaven. Teach the child that God is the Creator of all our world and the starry worlds we see at night in the sky. If parents are willing to take the time to explain that God watches over those who love him, the child will begin to understand the omnipresence of God, and as a rule will accept the fact that although God is everywhere, he still is, in a most personal way, close to those who can become his children.

THE PROBLEM OF SIN

Sin is a violation of the will of God as revealed in the Scriptures. It is not the same as being naughty. The parent should help the child to see the consequences of deliberately sinning against God's revealed will. But at all times the parent should communicate God's sorrow over sin.

A child must reach the age of accountability before he can understand his personal sin. Naughtiness can be shown to be undesirable much earlier by adapting penalties to fit behavior. The ideal form of penalty is self-enforcing consequences. "Johnny, if you are cruel to the cat, it won't be able to live here anymore because we do not have cruelty in our home." If cruelty continues, give the cat away! Let actions bring their own consequences rather than arbitrary punishments.

Spankings may at times be necessary for the child's will to be made submissive. But spankings should never be imposed in anger—only in sorrow. Never threaten the child with God's wrath because of the child's misbehavior. He must learn this later, and even then without the emotion of anger. He must see the consequences of disobeying the plainly understood will of God. But of course, we must teach the child what the will of God is, by reading the Scriptures and explaining them apart from the heat of emotion.

The child learns to lie as soon as he can speak if his parents threaten him with punishment. Parents are responsible for much lying on the part of children when they fail to deal with them lovingly and objectively. To back the child into a corner and leave him no protection except punishment from his naughtiness, disobedience, or carelessness, is to invite him to lie. Parents too often do this and then also punish the child for lying! The child figures a lie is better than punishment for his misdeed—who knows, he may get away with it this time!

But this is counterproductive to both parents and children. Older children sometimes must be left defenseless if they use false excuses so they can own up to their serious guilt. But this should be a rare occasion or it will encourage "trickiness" and deception. Just remember, self-protection is a natural human defense. The lie is the easiest way to maintain self-preservation. Given little occasion for this emotion to exhibit itself, the child will learn to prefer the truth!

THE KNOWLEDGE OF SPIRITUAL TRUTH

How much theology can a child absorb? Only as much as he can relate to the level of his knowledge and experience. But he must be taught certain basic doctrines as soon as he can understand them.

Truth is an early concept understandable to the child. While he cannot always be objective about truth as a concept, and while he may have difficulty discerning the difference between truth and imagination, he has little difficulty in recognizing an outright lie. Parents should handle imaginary statements with humor, but malicious lies should not be permitted to stand unchallenged. To let the child think he has "gotten away" with an outright lie is to reinforce this pattern of response.

Children do not "need" to lie if they know there is always a loving parent to understand. Part of that "understanding" is for the parent to explain the evil consequence inherent in lying and to explain that God has created the universe and governs it by truth. Jesus said, "I am the way, the *truth* and the life."

(1) The first theology a child can learn is the theology of truth and its value to God and himself.

(2) The second step is recognizing the value of kindness, especially the lovingkindness of God, through first understanding the love of parents.

(3) The third is the virtue of obedience. As children must obey their parents, so they must obey God. Care should be taken to see

that the order of this doctrine is stressed. The threat of God's displeasure should be sparingly mentioned—and never brought up apart from his love and justice. Yet, neither should the chastisement of God for sin be overlooked or ignored.

CHILDREN OF MEN AND CHILDREN OF GOD

It is foundational to Christianity that the Christian view of man be imparted early. That view is that children are born physically as offspring of the human race. God is the Creator and mankind is his creation—hence, all humans are his *creatures*.

Jesus plainly taught that it is not through physical birth that people become children of God. God is their Creator, not their Father. His fatherhood is granted to those who receive Christ as their personal Savior.

This statement of Christian truth, which is not commonly understood, is extremely vital. The popularly understood concept is that all people are children of God. This mistaken doctrine is often stated as, "The brotherhood of man under the fatherhood of God." Men *are* indeed brothers as fellow creatures. But God is not the Father of all men—only of those who have experienced the "second birth" which makes them his children.

Let us be very sure of this. If your children are mistakenly taught that they are God's children by virtue of their flesh and blood birth, they will see no need of a new or second "spiritual" birth. What would be the point of regeneration if the first birth were enough?

Check this doctrine in your own Bible. Be sure to note to *whom* a given verse of Scripture refers. For example, when it says "we," the verse usually means the writer, a Christian apostle, and his readers who are already regenerated Christians. It never means mankind as a whole or any "unsaved" person.

Now we are ready to demonstrate from Scripture that the statements given here represent a consistent position with no exceptions or variations.

> 1. Jesus answered and said unto him, Verily, verily, I say unto thee, Except a man be born again, he cannot see the kingdom of God (John 3:3).
>
> That which is born of the flesh is flesh; and that which is born of the Spirit is spirit (John 3:6).

Marvel not that I said unto thee, Ye must be born again (John 3:7).

2. That is, They which are the children of the flesh, these are not the children of God: but the children of the promise are counted for the seed (Rom. 9:8).

And it shall come to pass, that in the place where it was said unto them, Ye are not my people; there shall they be called the children of the living God (Rom. 9:26).

3. And that ye put on the new man, which after God is created in righteousness and true holiness (Eph. 4:24).

4. For ye are all the children of God by faith in Christ Jesus (Gal. 3:26).

5. But as many as received him, to them gave he power to become the sons of God, even to them that believe on his name. Which were born, not of blood, nor of the will of the flesh, nor of the will of man, but of God (John 1:12, 13).

Do not be content to merely read this. If you really wish to bring a child to know God, you have life's most serious task on your hands. Go to your Bible and read each of the above Scripture references for yourself!

To translate this great truth into your child's understanding is, of course, necessary. You must teach the child to address God as Father only after he is old enough and has experienced the second birth. This teaching may seem to be difficult emotionally, but we are dealing, not with sentiment, but with the precious soul of the child. The child looks forward someday to being able to call God "our Father in heaven." The anticipation of this privilege will prepare the child and make him eager to reach that great moment. Of course, he must be old enough to understand this rather complex doctrine, but it is easier than you might suppose. To suggest an appropriate age is impossible. That depends upon the amount of early Christian training in the home and his own mental and moral maturity. The age of accountability may range from six to twelve years.

There is simply no chance at all of a child getting to know God without the "new birth." He may and should very early know *about* God. But he cannot know God except through receiving Christ as his own Savior and Lord.

THE CHILD AND THE CHURCH

From his earliest days, the child should see the church as one of his familiar homes. Never should school or schoolwork be allowed to take precedence over church. The public school prepares the child for a relatively short social life. The church prepares him for eternity. A child is quick to discern which is more important by which has first place in his life and in his parents' lives.

The school offers both good and bad influences. There he will learn skepticism, worldliness, and peer group values, as well as his ABCs. Social pressures encountered at the high school age usually provide the first serious competition to a child's spiritual values. Will he be strong enough to face them victoriously? Only if he has a firm loyalty of *his own* to the church. You cannot build this loyalty in the child simply by dropping him off at Sunday school occasionally.

He must see that after his regeneration *he is the church*. The church (local assembly) is not something apart from himself which belongs to the older generation. It is *his*, too! His spiritual fulfillment and service are dependent upon the church.

Many parents take a casual attitude toward the church. Like tennis or family outings, it becomes one possible choice among many each weekend. The child cannot be fooled by this. It is a lesson which he will learn all too well! Remember Ephesians 5:25, "Christ . . . loved the church, and gave himself for it." For parents to do less than this would be to rob the child of the greatest influence for God in the world. Regular church attendance should not be an option any more than regular attendance at school is left to a whim. Never criticize the church in the presence of children without constructive and loyal suggestions as to how you can help change it for the better.

Children should be taught early to tithe all earned income to the church. Many a teenager is held true to God through difficult years by maintaining the habit of giving the tithe (10 percent of earned income). It should not be taught as a duty, but as one of the reasons God gives us the power to earn money. To give money to the church is to give of one's self, time, talents, and work in a negotiable form; for that is what money is, a part of one's *life* in a form that can be spent or given.

THE CHILD AND THE BIBLE

Little children should get to know the great stories of the Bible. Very early they should hear the Bible read aloud. Daily devotions, sometimes from devotional books, greatly help children get to know God. Each child should have his own Bible as soon as he is old enough to read. Modern special versions are good, but so is the King James Bible, which is unsurpassed in its literary style. But the Bible should be explained by asking the child questions and inviting his participation in discussing the Scriptures as they are read in family devotions.

NINE
HOW TO TEACH
YOUR CHILD
ABOUT SEX

Our bookstores are overflowing with "How To" books: how to be successful, to have a happy marriage, to be a powerful speaker, to think positively, to influence others, to get ahead in business, to solve all your problems, etc.

Of course, there is really only one Book which contains all of these answers—the Bible. If people would only learn this one simple lesson, they could live happy, productive lives and rear happy, well-adjusted families. The Bible is *the* Book of answers, answers to all mysteries, answers to all petitions, to all human ills, to all human quandaries and perplexities.

In considering the subject of sex, then, we should turn first to the Bible. We note in the first chapter of Genesis that God created heaven and earth and the firmament and night and day and the sun and moon and stars; then he created the creatures of the earth and seas, and said to them: "Be fruitful and multiply."

And then God created man and woman and said to them: "Be fruitful and multiply and replenish the earth." And so God instituted marriage and sex so that the earth would be replenished, both with all the creatures he had created and with mankind. And so sex was divinely instituted, and as with all other things instituted by God, it is to be used only in accordance with his plan and laws.

Sex is a normal human need, but far too often we see sex polluted and made unclean, just as we see the pollution of the air and water and the earth and the other gifts God gave us. The gift of sex was misused by Tamar and Judah and David and many others, but perhaps it is abused and made evil today more than any time since Sodom and Gomorrah.

Ours is a society obsessed with sex. Sex is blazoned everywhere—in our newspapers and magazines, on the covers of books and records, on signboards and movie marquees, and, worst of all, on our television screens. Sex is sold not only in houses of prostitution but also in so-called "massage parlors," which line the streets in many cities. It is sold in advertising and commercials that intrude upon the minds of our children—along with cigarettes, toothpaste, deodorants, shaving cream, perfume, etc.

Pearl Buck observed that "no people in the world have changed as much in the past twenty years as Americans, and nowhere is the change more apparent than in our ethics of sex." What she says is profoundly and tragically true. Our society is saturated with sex—the wrong kind of sex—and our children are in greater danger than perhaps any other generation has been of becoming victims of this sex mania. This situation makes it all the more imperative that parents assume the responsibility of teaching their children about sex in its true perspective.

THE RIGHT TO KNOW

Children become curious about sex at an early age—in our time, earlier than ever before. They become curious long before they have—or should have—any specific knowledge about sex functions.

Parents should keep one fact strongly in mind: the child has a *right* to know about sex. A child has the right to know why he or she is male or female, what being of one sex or the other will mean, what will be expected of him, what kinds of problems may arise related to sex. And it is the responsibility of parents to provide the right answers in the right way: forthrightly, naturally, and accurately.

And as it is the right of the child to know about sex, it is his right to know the truth and all the truth about it—not just the physical aspects, not just the snares, not just the disagreeable points. The child has a right to know—and the parents have a duty to teach—that sexuality is a gift of God, given to carry on a sacred purpose, love and procreation. And this role of sex will *never* be successfully or satisfactorily taught in a classroom by teachers, counselors, or advisers who believe that sex is merely physical, experimental, and "just for fun." This is the danger of sex education in schools or anywhere outside the home, and it is tragic that so many parents are abdicating their own responsibilities in this vital area.

Young people who learn about sex without being told of God's part in it are like a person who learns to drive a car but does not know the rules of the road. He will drive anywhere—on the sidewalks, on private property, at any speed, and with no regard for his safety or that of others. Even a driver who knows the rules but does not know the reasons for them will not be a good driver. He will assume that it is all right to go through a stop sign or a red light—as long as no one sees him. Young people should learn that they must use this gift of sex as God intended, not from fear, not just to avoid "getting caught," but from love of God and the desire to please and obey him.

Children have a right to know the beauty of sex, when it is a part of love and marriage. They should be aware of the consequences of using sex for wrong purposes, but instruction should not dwell on ugliness, misery, disease, and all of the evil by-products of sexual promiscuity and misuse. They should know that sex, as a part of Christian marriage, is a beautiful and holy part of this life.

THE DUTY TO TEACH

A parent may not shirk the duty of proper sex instruction to children any more than he may shirk the duty to provide for them. And above all, he must not attempt to delegate this task to others. No one, not the most highly accredited "expert," the most highly touted "authority," can be substituted for a parent in meeting this responsibility.

One stark fact ought to stand out in the parents' minds. Your child is the creation of your sex. As partners, your sexual desire and love created this child. Above all things, then, is it not your duty to help him understand this great and holy force which produced him, so that when the time comes for him to marry, he will know all the wonder and joy of his sexuality?

HOW TO BEGIN

Be a Good Example. The best teaching is by example. If a picture is worth a hundred words, a good example is worth 10,000. It is, indeed, a picture brought to life. How better to teach a child the beauty of a good marriage than by example—by living a good marriage? A mother said to me: "Judy has come home several times after visiting girl friends and said to me, 'Oh, Mother, I feel so sorry for Pam [or Mary or Kim]. Her parents fight all the time. Her mom says awful things about her father. I couldn't stand living in a house like that.'"

How could Pam's mother possibly teach her about a good marriage? How could her parents teach her about sex if she hears them quarreling about it; if her parents occupy separate rooms; if she hears her mother talking on the phone and deriding sex?

How can parents hope to teach their children about God, about Christianity, if they do not pray, do not go to church, do not give to the church, are selfish and self-centered, hypocritical, and without sympathy or compassion?

Children have a wonderful instinct for detecting hypocrisy and insincerity. They are not easily taken in by words when the actions are entirely different. Your attitudes will show through what you say and the result will be worse than if you had said nothing. Children resent hypocrisy and they resent being taken as dupes or fools. "How can they think I am so stupid?" will be the reaction of children whose parents "sweet talk" them about good conduct when their example is completely opposite.

Children will observe and listen. But it is not only the reassurance of the love between parents that a child needs. It is parental love for him and a realization of their need for *his* love as well. This need not be expressed in words. It may be shown by tender concern, in smiles, in looks, and in actions; by the tone of voice, the interest and approval given to him, the expressed curiosity about his daily affairs—and especially by encouragement and support during crises. And parents must also be receptive to the child's love and concern. Love is strictly a two-way proposition, whether between husband and wife, parent and child, or God and man.

Both Parents Are Responsible. In some families one parent is apt to try to delegate sex education to the other. The father may say to the children: "Talk to your mother, this is her department." Or the mother may say: "I'll talk to Jane, but you must talk to John."

Both are wrong. The responsibility is joint and indivisible. Both parents must participate. A "woman's viewpoint" is not enough, nor is "the male angle" on sex adequate. Furthermore, the outlook on sex is so strongly personalized and colored by experience and personal qualities that no one person can convey a completely objective message. Parents should talk together and work together as they do in other aspects of instruction. They will scarcely have a more vital joint project than this.

This is not to say that parents should always speak to the child together. This will usually not be the case. But each must be available and ready. The child should feel free to ask questions of either parent, as he does in other matters. This should be the case in the beginning and earlier stages of discussions about sex. Later on, of course, it will be perfectly natural and proper for a daughter to talk more with the mother, as problems become more intimate and specialized. And the son will feel more comfortable seeking the counsel of his father. Yet both parents must remain interested and available for consultation.

Sex Means Self-discipline. The problems of sex, of course, are simply part of the general area of discipline and self-control that a child must begin to learn as soon as he or she is out of the cradle— and that each individual must continue learning all through life. Man is mortal and weak; he is flesh as well as spirit; he is prone to sin and transgression. That is why God instituted the Ten Commandments and the moral law. Flesh and the devil are constantly—and subtly—calling on man to yield to his base desires, to become purely a physical, animal creature and disavow his spiritual nature. The important thing to teach the child is persistence of the temptations that will beset him so that he will be fortified with the knowledge and discipline to resist.

Discipline is not learned in a classroom like ABCs. There is the classroom discipline of order and acceptable conduct, but personal self-discipline is the long, slow, continuous process of coping with day-to-day situations. It is learning about duty, obligations, respect for the rights of others, submission to the laws of God, obedience to parents and persons in authority. Discipline is, of course, a great deal more than what is involved in relationships with other people. Discipline is learning to deal properly with one's own instinct. If each of us were to be guided entirely by instinct, the world would be chaos. Children must learn that certain instincts must be suppressed or governed in proper ways. The earliest lesson of this kind is toilet training.

WHEN TO BEGIN

When asked, "When shall I begin to tell my child about sex?" I usually answer, "You already have." A doctor friend told me of a mother bringing in a boy for an examination. After the examination, she asked when she should begin to talk to her son about sex. The doctor asked how old he was. "Six years old." "Madam," the doctor said, "I would begin as soon as possible, because you are six years late already."

A child may be too young to comprehend biology, but he is quite capable of learning about life and love in the home, and later in the neighborhood, even in preschool days. With so many working mothers, a great many children will have their sex and moral education commenced in a child care center or preschool. How well qualified will the teachers or aides in those places be?

Long before a child understands where he came from or how he got here, he is learning about emotions and intense feelings from what happens about him in his home, in the homes of other relatives or friends, in the park, at the beach, etc. Your own attitudes toward love, life, your mate, your children—these are the beginning of your child's sex education.

When the child is ready for specific information, you must be ready too. You will tell him how a mother must care for a baby in her own body before it is born, how a baby grows and develops in the womb. How to tell the story will be for you to decide, but helps are available.

Sex has two vocabularies—a dirty vocabulary and a scientific vocabulary. Sex organs have correct, scientific names as well as crude ones. Parents must accept and use the proper sex terms to explain sex, although they may not come naturally at first.

Sex explanations should be succinct and accurate—not curt

or unduly prolonged. A spontaneous question is not an invitation to a lecture. The child wants an explanation, not doctoral dissertation. Be matter-of-fact, patient, forthright, and completely honest. If a girl wants to know why she must keep her dress down or a boy wants to know what girls wear under their dresses, there are short, simple, and sufficient answers—answers as natural as why girls and boys go to different public bathrooms.

Your Christian bookstores will have some splendid resources for you, such as *Understanding Your Children,* by Dr. Clyde M. Narramore, for the younger child; and Dr. Norman Vincent Peale's *Sin, Sex and Self-Control,* a practical and inspiring guide to the challenge of the problems of young people. These two Christian leaders affirm the biblical concept of sexuality. They will strengthen your own convictions so that you are equipped to pass a great heritage on to your children in a day when too many of the old rules of behavior seem abandoned.

It is also helpful to buy for your library the books that express your own attitudes and beliefs. Then add new books as they appear from time to time. As your child becomes older and is interested in the subject, he will be able to turn to these and read for himself.

Children resist being preached to or talked at. Therefore, if you hope to give advice or instruction there must first be a basis for mutual friendship and understanding. Always, your child needs assurance that you have faith in him and in his living up to that faith. This does not mean that parents should not adhere to rules, for a child wishes his parents to act as kind but firm adults. Especially as a young person enters his teens, he does not want a mother or father to act like one of his contemporaries. But to say, in the matter of sex offenses, "If you ever do this again . . ." and then threaten your child, is to open a chasm in your relationship which later you may not be able to bridge.

In place of threats, what is needed? First, an explanation should be made of why the home requires certain behavior— that it is for the child's protection, to make him a happier, better person with self-esteem and the respect of others. This is a challenge to him to be his best self. Dr. Haim G. Ginott, in his book *Between Parent and Child,* has given us a helpful rule to follow for our children at any age level, but particularly as the teen days arrive. It is: "Parents must be allies in the child's struggle for control of such impulses. By setting limits, the parents offer help to the child. Besides stopping dangerous conduct, the limit conveys a silent message: 'You don't have to be afraid of your impulses. I won't let you go too far. I love you. You are safe.'"

YOUR TIME IS SHORT

"The final year or two of the preteen stage is probably the last real chance you'll have to guide your child," warns Dr. Eugene Scheimann, M.D. The years slip past so swiftly that what were formerly "small" problems now loom as "large" ones. When your child is of high school or college age his daily environment may "percolate" with resentment against tradition and conduct which is demanded by parents. He is faced with problems; "Is this a new, broader, more-fun way to live? If the 'new math' is better, why not the 'new morals'?" "Are my parents always right?"

A prosecutor who reported that he read to the jury the entire book *Tropic of Cancer* noted, "The book was filthy. For about twenty-five pages the jurors were mortified. They looked anywhere but at me, humiliated. But I noticed then as I read on, they increasingly relaxed, captively accepted the new morality, and my words became to them commonplace." This is the creeping paralysis of evil.

Because movies, books, or slides are sanctioned by a school board or a particular principal or faculty does not necessarily make them suitable for your child or others. Constant vigilance is the parents' privilege and duty. Parents, school officials, and board members gathered at Garden Grove, California, for a public showing of the family life education films to be used by the district. Seventeen films were shown to a standing-room-only crowd. These were some of the reactions reported by the newspaper. A mother of three boys said: "I've been opposed to this sex education all along, because they are teaching our children that sexual intercourse is normal and natural—as long as they trust a person." A city councilman, father of four, commented: "I tell my kids something is wrong and their teachers tell them it's right. From what I've seen now I'm going to do everything I can to stop this program."

Since the United States government spends millions upon millions of your tax dollars to teach your child about sex, you have a right to ask that some "moral," or "spiritual," principles be included. These are some of the inalienable rights by which you were endowed by your Creator. Until the United States government is ready to deny its Constitution, it cannot deny you such privileges. The Supreme Court upheld the right of the astronauts to read from Genesis; you and your family have a right to believe that "God created man in his image," and that the school has no right to degrade that image or to deny God's commandments.

Parents may fear to oppose programs or materials used by schools because their child will have to bear taunts from fellow students and even the scorn or retribution of some teacher. If this is the result of your sensible, tactful, polite complaint about a matter so important to your child's future, then you must go beyond the teacher and take steps to insure your child's constitutional rights. We cannot impose religious beliefs upon others, but others must not be allowed to impose their humanism, atheism, or pagan views upon your child in the guise of updating morality. Your very actions in protest will be part of your child's learning process about life, courage, and conviction.

TROUBLE ON THE HOME FRONT

While you may be winning wars in the community, often you will feel that you are losing battles on the home front. Your teenager comes home with many newfound ideas, and hopefully he is vocal about them. If these concepts come from the pinnacle of the educational platform, he will be most impressed. If you disagree with them, you represent "repression" to his new desire to conform for the sake of popularity, if not for "freedom." Tempers can flare and small rifts can become chasms. Are you ready for questions like these:

>Sex is just another appetite like hunger or thirst; what's wrong with satisfying it?

> Why feel guilty about sex? That is Puritanism. Why not shake off the neurotic inhibitions that are not in tune with today's world?
>
> Love is the important thing. Between any two people, expressing love in any way is better than the "up-tight" attitude of parents.

Many parents do not meet these questions head-on. There is timidity caused by fear of losing the child's love. Some "look the other way," pretending to themselves that their child is not taking steps into immorality. But if you are playing such games, your young people know it. What is the answer? Hopefully, your child is still in the talking stage and not trying to justify his own conscience about his own misdeeds. Hopefully, these questions will arise in family conversational give-and-take before the young person gets too emotionally involved.

Your child should have been armed to stand his ground on his own decisions, through his own choice, against the harmful and the immoral. In early youth, idealism runs high and commitments to uphold ideals can be made early, before the onslaught of temptation comes. How it comes out will depend on how much your child has learned about self-discipline, self-control, and self-mastery. But these can only be nurtured in an atmosphere of self-esteem.

Waiting until a sex crisis is at hand does not take into account the power of sex. For example, parents who provide swimming lessons do so to teach their child to respect the power of the ocean and undertows as yet unknown to him. Yet they may fail to explain the future potency of sexual stimulation. Guidelines set early prepare the child to meet these forces.

Is a sex crisis the time to tell your young contender that sex outside of marriage is contrary to the will of God? It may be, but this should not be the first time. Along with this there must be an appeal to his newfound power of rationalization and his respect for facts and science, as well as idealism.

> Only when we convince people, both rationally and emotionally, of these things; only when we supply clear evidence

that in casual sex the game is not worth the candle, will we be able to reverse the trend toward anarchy in this, the most intimate of all relationships.

It is the insistence, buttressed by twenty centuries of human experience, that the rewards of sexual control are worth having and that the penalties of sexual license sooner or later are grim, painful, destructive and negative. —Norman Vincent Peale, *Sin, Sex and Self-Control.*

The parent faced with these arguments remembers that *don'ts* alone have not worked in the past, in securing the child's acceptable behavior. It is time for him to give the orders based on a moral code he has built, on your guidance, and on the guidance of his religion. You may find for him some reinforcement from scientists.

Dr. George W. Corner, author of *"Science and Sex Ethics" (Saturday Evening Post,* Oct. 10, 1969) wrote:

If now, after long experience as an investigator of sex and reproduction, I assume the role of moralist, it is because I have seen nothing in my field of science to invalidate the age-old ideal of our culture—the permanent union of a man and woman in marriage; upon this ideal, with tolerance and understanding gained through the study of natural human needs, we can still base our sexual ethics.

And what is the answer to the question, "Isn't sex just another appetite?" The answer is all that you have previously discussed with your child about sex as a fulfillment of our highest hopes and ideals. "Protective love" should have been a part of every daughter's sex education from the time she first tenderly played with her dolls. "Protective love" should be the shining dream and evidence of a young man's manhood, the proof of his character and honor. Young people truly in love ask, "Can I entrust my life and our children's lives to this one I love?" Love has been misunderstood. Love is never animalistic nor egocentric—this is purely an expression of lust. You can help you child realize what young people miss who trade the spiritual and physical expression of love in marriage for sex-for-fun.

APPENDIX
GOD'S
SEX EDUCATION
PROGRAM

Compiled by Crestwood Concerned Parents
P.O. Box No. 1 — Dearborn Heights, MI 48127

Modern-day sex education is presented with a nontaboo, open approach not based on the Bible. This means the restraining influence of God's Word in connection with man's sexual behavior will not be used as a sexual guideline, because the United States Supreme Court says the Bible may not be read in the schools.

God's Word has provided a good guideline for man's sexual behavior for over 6000 years and now we are being given a sex education program without this guideline. The results of this kind of a program will be a further increase in illegitimate sexual activity, as there has been in other areas where this type of program has been taught. The result of increased improper sexual activity is the destruction of the family unit which is a strong source of security for most of us.

Our problems of divorce rate, homosexuality, venereal disease, etc., are caused by a neglect of teaching the following Scriptures at home and in school sex education classes. This is the only way to correct the ill that is upon us.

GOD'S DISFAVOR WITH IMMORALITY
One thing that God abhors is sexual immorality. The ancient nation of Israel was broken up due to this condition. The entire book of Hosea tells the story. B.C. 785.

Hosea 2:4
Hosea 4:1, 2
Hosea 4:6, 11
Hosea 9:17
Nahum 1:7, 8
Nahum 2:13
Nahum 3:4, 5

Fornication
Exodus 22:16
Deuteronomy 22:21
Deuteronomy 23:17
Proverbs 5:20-23
Proverbs 6:26
Matthew 15:18, 19
Romans 1:29-32
1 Corinthians 5:9
1 Corinthians 6:9, 11
1 Corinthians 6:18-20
1 Corinthians 7:2
Galatians 5:19-26
Galatians 6:7-9
Ephesians 5:1-8
Ephesians 5:9-17
Colossians 3:1-10
Colossians 3:18-21
1 Thessalonians 4:3
Jude 7
Revelation 2:21, 22

Love and Marriage
Song of Solomon 8:7
Ephesians 5:21-24
Ephesians 5:25-33

Adultery
Exodus 20:14, 17
Leviticus 18:20
Leviticus 20:1, 10-12

Leviticus 20:14, 21
Deuteronomy 5:18
Deuteronomy 22:22
Job 24:15
Proverbs 6:29-35
Malachi 3:5, 6
Matthew 19:18
Romans 13:9
Hebrews 13:4
2 Peter 2:14

Harlotry
Proverbs 7:10-12
Proverbs 7:25-27
Proverbs 23:27, 28
Ecclesiastes 7:26

Lust
Matthew 5:28
1 Corinthians 10:6, 8
Galatians 5:24
Titus 2:12-15
1 Peter 2:11
2 Peter 1:4
1 John 2:15-17
Jude 18

*Sodomy—Lesbianism-
Homosexuality*
Exodus 22:19
Leviticus 18:22-24
Leviticus 20:13
Leviticus 20:15, 16
Romans 1:26-28

Nakedness
Leviticus 18:17
Leviticus 20:17, 19, 21
Leviticus 20:23, 24, 26

Rape
Deuteronomy 22:25

Prostitution
Leviticus 19:29

*Rules for
the Priests of Israel*
Leviticus 21:9, 13, 14

Related
Proverbs 12:2, 4
Proverbs 15:3
Proverbs 22:6
Proverbs 31:10-12
Proverbs 31:26-30

Ecclesiastes 12:1
Romans 6:9-23
Romans 12:1, 2
Romans 12:21
Romans 13:14
1 Corinthians 3:16, 17
1 Corinthians 10:31
2 Corinthians 7:1
1 Thessalonians 5:22
Hebrews 4:12, 13

Conclusion
Psalm 1
Psalm 119:9-16
Proverbs 14:34

TERMS

Adultery	Sexual intercourse outside of marriage with a partner who is married to someone else.
Fornication	Sexual intercourse by unmarried persons.
Lewd	Characterized by inciting to lust.
Lust	Overpowering lawless sexual desire or covetousness.
Masturbation	Sexual manipulation for self-gratification.
Obscene	Offensive to modesty or decency; indecent; lewd; abominable; disgusting; repulsive.
Pornography	Obscene literature or art.
Sodomy	Man-to-man or man-to-animal sex relations.
Whore	Prostitute, harlot.
Whoremonger	One who frequents prostitutes.